Unleash the Resiliator Within

Resilience: A Handbook for Individuals

Also by Karen Ferris:
Game On! Change is Constant
Unleash the Resiliator Within—Resilience: A Handbook for Leaders

RESILIENCE: A HANDBOOK FOR INDIVIDUALS

KAREN FERRIS

About the author

Karen Ferris is an unashamed organizational change management rebel with a cause. She likes to challenge the status quo but only when her reason for doing so is defensible.

Karen began her working life in IT but she has spent a large part of her career in the IT service management space where she is recognized globally for her expertise and insight.

As someone who is continually focused on the people side of change, Karen authored a publication titled *Balanced Diversity: A Portfolio Approach to Organizational Change* in 2010.

She considered herself an accidental author back then. She stumbled across a framework for embedding change, set out to write a white paper about it and ended up with a book. That was the moment she was propelled into the world of organizational change management.

In 2019, she published her second book *Game On! Change is Constant: Tactics to Win When Leading Change is Everyone's Business*. Karen is a sought after international keynote speaker, coach, mentor, facilitator and trainer.

Born in Liverpool, UK, she emigrated to Australia in 1998. She lives with her wife, Breed, in Melbourne. She is an avid Liverpool Football Club supporter, an Elvis fan, has an obsession with shoes, and is a self-confessed arctophile—you might want to Google that.

Contents

Introduction

Constant, volatile, uncertain, complex and ambiguous (VUCA) change is a reality. As competition and consumer demands increase, and as digital disruption intensifies, organizations and the individuals within them need to stop talking about resistance to change and start talking about resilience in the face of change.

We cannot control or manage change anymore. We must embrace the uncertainty and be ready to sense and respond, adapt and flex, diverge and converge, and be truly agile—all at a pace we've never experienced before.

In this environment, we need people at every level of an organization who can deal with the difficulties, demands, uncertainties and pressures of constant change without burning out. We need individuals who don't just bounce back from setbacks, but bounce forward and make good out of the situation. We need individuals who embrace change and are ready to adapt and reposition with confidence and self-reliance.

I have named these people, Resiliators. Resiliators thrive in the face of constant change; they possess a multitude of superpowers in order to do so.

This handbook is for individuals at all levels of an organization who need to develop resilience. It will equip you with the superpowers to say 'Game On!' in the face of constant change.

This handbook is also a companion to the *interactive Resiliator platform*, which is available to organizations in need of developing individual resilience across the entire workforce.

≈ ≈ ≈

The companion publication *Unleash the Resiliator Within—Resilience: A Handbook for Leaders* describes the superpowers of anyone who leads others and whose role, therefore, is to maintain and sustain resilience in others so that they can say 'Game On!' in the face of constant change.

The Resiliator

What does the Resiliator look like?

In a nutshell, you are observing the Resiliator if you see the following traits.

Resiliators:

- Accept ambiguity and embrace uncertainty. They recognize and accept that they don't always have all the answers.

- Act thoughtfully. They assess a situation and respond to it rather than react to it. They are problem-solvers and carefully evaluate a situation before they try to resolve it.

- Manage their emotions. They have emotional intelligence.

- Are self-aware. They have a clear understanding of their strengths and weaknesses, thoughts and beliefs, motivations and emotions.

- Maintain a positive outlook with realistic optimism.

- Connect, collaborate and build networks.

- Operate with empathy. They are sensitive to the feelings of others and are able to demonstrate compassion and understanding.

- Maintain a growth mindset. They are accepting of failure as a means of learning and development.

- Are confident in their abilities and will make good use of their strengths while not focusing on their weaknesses.

Resilience

There are two sides to the resilience coin.

1. Equipping all individuals with the various superpowers they need to be resilient in the face of constant change.

2. Equipping those leading others with the knowledge and capability to maintain and sustain resilience in others.

This handbook deals with the former. The companion handbook, *Unleash the Resiliator Within—Resilience: A Handbook for Leaders* deals with the latter.

Benefits for the individual

As an individual, there are numerous benefits to being resilient. These include:

- Better physical and mental health.
- Improved cognitive functioning.
- Maintained inner calm in stressful situations.
- Life perceived as a series of challenges not problems.
- Stability in the face of a crisis.
- Capacity to thrive in situations of high demand and ongoing pressure.
- Ability to recover quickly from setbacks.
- Failures and setbacks are seen as learning opportunities.
- Reduced burnout.
- Increased sense of community.

How can you afford not to invest in yourself to become more resilient?

Benefits for the organization

Employees who are not resilient, soon become disengaged and either tune out or leave the organization.

According to Gallup's 2017 report *State of the Global Workplace*, 85% of adults worldwide are not engaged or are actively disengaged in the workplace.[1]

The report states that organizations in the top quartile of employee engagement, as opposed to those in the bottom quartile, realize benefits in the following areas:

- 17% higher productivity
- 21% higher profitability
- 59% lower turnover (in low-turnover organizations)
- 24% lower turnover (in high-turnover organizations)
- 41% lower absenteeism.

Gallup and other reports provide the cost of employee disengagement by country. These are some of the figures:

- Germany is 214.7 to 287.1 billion euros per year.[2]
- United States is half a trillion dollars per year.[3]
- UK is 52–70 billion pounds per year.[4]

Return on investment

Spending money on building a resilient workforce returns dividends. Employee engagement increases and turnover decreases. Absenteeism and sick leave decrease, and productivity and motivation increase, which leads to increased profitability.

In 2019, the World Health Organization published an information sheet titled *Mental Health in the Workplace*. It stated "Depression and anxiety have a significant economic impact; the estimated cost to the global economy is US$ 1 trillion per year in lost productivity."[5]

Back in 2014, Price Waterhouse Coopers (PwC) undertook a return on investment analysis for Australian employers who wanted to create mentally healthy workplaces. To achieve that objective, PwC teamed up with Beyond Blue, The National Mental Health Commission, academic experts in mental health and the workplace, and further representatives from different workplace contexts.

The report *Creating a Mentally Healthy Workplace: Return on Investment Analysis* states that "through the successful implementation of an effective action to create a mentally healthy workplace, organizations, on average, can expect a positive return on investment (ROI) of 2.3."[6]

That is a return of 2.3 dollars for every dollar spent.

The World Health Organization also stated the ROI in mental health initiatives: "For every US$ 1 put into scaled up treatment for common mental disorders, there is a return of US$ 4 in improved health and productivity."[7]

Consequences

In 2019, the Victorian Government in Australia introduced workplace manslaughter laws.

The Victorian Workplace Safety Legislation Amendment (Workplace Manslaughter and Other Matters) Act 2019 includes fines of up to $100,000 penalty units currently equating to $16,522,000 for bodies corporate, and jail terms of up to 20 years for company officers who negligently cause a work-related death."[8]

So, if you are a 'company officer' who is found negligent in taking action to prevent mental health issues in the workplace that result in suicide, you could be facing up to two decades in jail and a hefty fine to boot.

There are other states in Australia with similar legislation.

In December 2019, three top corporate executives at French telecommunications company France Télécom (now Orange) were convicted of "collective moral harassment" and "institutional harassment" for creating a toxic work environment that led to 19 employee suicides and a further 12 employees who attempted to take their own lives. Former CEO, Didier Lombard, was sentenced to one year in jail (of which 8 months were suspended), along with a €15,000 fine. His former deputy, Louis-Pierre Wenès, and human resources director, Olivier Barberot, received the same sentence and fine. Four other executives were given four-month suspended sentences and €5,000 fines.[9]

Can your organization afford *not* to take action?

Resilience and superpowers

It's all about the superpowers. In the face of constant change, we all need a range of superpowers at hand that will help us to be resilient. Only when the required superpower(s) are unleashed, can we thrive in the face of relentless and uncertain change.

Individual resilience is critical when the world around us is volatile, uncertain, complex and ambiguous. Resilience means we can adapt to difficult situations and not just survive but thrive. If we fail to adapt, the stress will overwhelm us, and we will suffer physically and mentally.

My Resiliator model shows all of the superpowers. We need these superpowers if we are to be resilient.

Each superpower can be used at any time. Whichever you choose will depend on the context and situation you are facing. Multiple superpowers can be used at the same time, and the choice will be subject to the needs of the individual.

For example, an individual may be faced with a dramatic change in direction after a period spent pursuing a particular outcome. They have no control over the external conditions driving the change in direction. This individual could go into lockdown, exhibit extremely angry behavior, blame others, lose control and become stressed.

The longer this situation or feeling exists increases the chance of adverse impacts on both mental and physical health. This is a situation that can be avoided.

The individual could select to use the superpowers of the Regulator, the Observer, the Reframer and the Collaborator

The Regulator regulates emotions and controls feelings. They regulate impulse and focus on tasks at hand—not the emotions.

They do not make a drama out of a crisis. They exercise emotional intelligence skills including stress tolerance and impulse control.

The Observer practices mindfulness. They are able to pause, stand back, observe and reflect. They can decenter stress and shift their perspectives. They focus on the present and calmly accept and acknowledge their emotions.

The Reframer looks at things from a different perspective. They view situations from different angles to give them more context, increase positivity, remove negativity and seek opportunity in the situation.

The Collaborator reaches out. They reach out for support (and offer it also). They seek out new relationships and build networks that will support collaboration. Effective collaboration enables a person to see the bigger picture.

By adopting these superpowers, the individual increases their ability to be resilient. Through application and practice, they unleash the Resiliator within.

Caution

It is important to note that you do not have to become an expert in utilizing all of the superpowers. You won't need all of them, all of the time.

Each time you use a superpower, you will become better at it. Many of the superpowers need practice, so the more you use them, the better you become.

You will choose the superpower(s) you believe will best meet your needs in any given situation. Just like any other superhero, you will use the superpower(s) best suited to overcome the challenge currently in front of you. You can mix and match the superpowers as needed.

We will look at each of the Resiliator superpowers available to you as an individual within your organization.

THE REGULATOR
STRESS TOLERANCE AND
IMPULSE CONTROL

THE SOLVER
EFFECTIVE PROBLEM SOLVING

THE REALISTIC OPTIMIST
BELIEVE IN CHANGE FOR THE BETTER

THE FUTURIST
LONG-TERM PERSPECTIVE

THE EMPATHIZER
AWARENESS OF OTHERS' FEELINGS,
NEEDS AND CONCERNS

THE CATEGORIZER
PRIORITIZATION AND FOCUS

THE ADAPTER
ADAPTATION TO CHANGE
AND UNCERTAINTY

THE THANKER
GRATITUDE

THE COLLABORATOR
WORKING WITH OTHERS TOWARD
SHARED GOALS

THE OBSERVER
SELF-OBSERVATION

THE ACHIEVER
SENSE OF PURPOSE

THE REVEALER
AUTHENTIC SELF

THE EXPLORER
LEARNING, PASSION AND
PERSEVERANCE

THE QUESTIONER
CHALLENGE THE STATUS QUO

THE CELEBRANT
CELEBRATION OF SUCCESS
AND FAILURE

THE REFRAMER
CHANGE PERSPECTIVE

THE EXPERIMENTER
INNOVATION FUELLED BY
EXPERIMENTATION

THE BELIEVER
SELF-BELIEF

THE HUMORIST
HUMOR AS A COPING MECHANISM

THE LISTENER
EFFECTIVE LISTENING

Meet the Resiliators

Throughout this handbook, we will look at how the following group of Resiliators have used their superpowers.

Maria, Taya, Charlie and Aditya work for ABC Corporation. ABC Corporation is a large fashion retailer.

Maria has been with the company for seven years, and she is a senior member of the marketing team.

Taya is only six months into her job, and she works in the customer contact center.

Charlie works in distribution, and he recently got promoted to team leader after 2 ½ years with the organization.

Aditya has the longest tenure. He joined the company 15 years ago. He works in the finance department.

ABC Corporation has undergone considerable change as the retail industry is faced with increasing competition and technological disruption. The speed of change is not decreasing.

Maria, Taya, Charlie and Aditya have all used the Resiliator superpowers to help them navigate constant change.

We will hear from each of them, in their own words, as we look at each superpower.

The Regulator

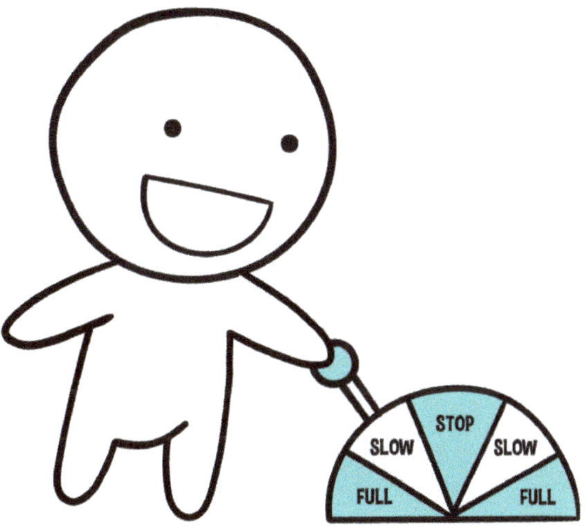

Superpower: Regulation

Note: Some content within this module has been reproduced from Working With Emotional Intelligence *with permission from author Daniel Goleman.*

The Regulator is able to regulate their emotions. They exercise stress tolerance and impulse control. They avoid turning a drama into a crisis and respond to situations rather than react to them. They don't allow their thoughts to cloud their judgment.

The Regulator will pause and reflect to increase their self-awareness. They take time and put in the effort to discover who they really are and become kind enough to accept their entire self—warts and all.

The Regulator exercises emotional intelligence.

Emotional intelligence

Daniel Goleman, an American psychologist, brought emotional intelligence to the forefront in his 1995 book *Emotional Intelligence: Why It Can Matter More Than IQ*.

Emotional intelligence is the ability to recognize and understand our own emotions, while also being able to recognize, understand and influence the emotions of others.

Having emotional intelligence helps to build relationships, reduce stress, defuse conflict and improve job satisfaction.

In his 1998 publication, *Working With Emotional Intelligence*, Goleman introduced the Emotional Competency Framework, which illustrates the relationship between five dimensions of emotional intelligence and 25 emotional competencies.

The dimensions are:

- Self-awareness
- Self-regulation
- Motivation (internal)
- Empathy
- Social skills.

Extensive research referenced within Goleman's body of work has shown that emotional intelligence competencies are twice as important than pure intellect and expertise in contributing to individual and organizational excellence.

It is not a requirement to master every competency in every dimension. Competencies come in clusters and will, in part, be driven by the nature of the job, the organization and the work being undertaken.

However, top performers will have mastered competencies from each of the five emotional intelligence dimensions and, therefore, have

strengths across the board. When they reach a critical mass from the entire set of competencies, they will emerge as outstanding.

The Regulator utilizes two of the emotional intelligence dimensions: self-awareness and self-regulation.

Self-awareness

The cornerstone of emotional intelligence is self-awareness. You can only change what you know. Self-awareness is about knowing yourself. According to Goleman, "Self-awareness concerns knowing one's internal states, preferences, resources, and intuitions."

The self-awareness dimension contains three competencies.

1. **Emotional awareness:** Recognizing one's emotions and their effects.
2. **Accurate self-assessment:** Knowing one's strengths and limits.
3. **Self-confidence:** A strong sense of one's self-worth and capabilities.

Emotional awareness

People will this competency:

- Know which emotions they are feeling and why.
- Realize the links between their feelings and what they think, do and say.
- Recognize how their feelings affect their performance.
- Have a guiding awareness of their values and goals.

Accurate self-assessment

People with this competency are:

- Aware of their strengths and weaknesses.
- Reflective: they learn from their experience.
- Open to candid feedback, new perspectives, continuous learning and self-development.

- Able to show a sense of humor and perspectives about themselves.

Self-confidence

People with this competency:

- Present themselves with self-assurance and have "presence".
- Can voice views that are unpopular and go out on a limb for what is right.
- Are decisive: they are able to make sound decisions despite uncertainties and pressures.

Self-regulation

Self-regulation is about having the ability to manage one's emotions, impulses and resources.

The self-regulation dimension contains five competencies.

1. Self-control: Keeping disruptive emotions and impulses in check.
2. Trustworthiness: Maintaining standards of honesty and integrity.
3. Conscientiousness: Taking responsibility for personal performance.
4. Adaptability: Flexibility in handling change.
5. Innovation: Being comfortable with novel ideas, approaches and new information.

Self-control

People with this competency:

- Manage their impulsive feelings and distressing emotions well.
- Stay composed, positive and unflappable in trying moments.
- Think clearly and stay focused under pressure.

Trustworthiness and conscientiousness

People with the competency of trustworthiness:

- Act ethically and are above reproach.
- Build trust through their reliability and authenticity.
- Admit their own mistakes and confront unethical actions in others.
- Take tough, principled stands even if they are unpopular.

People with the competency of conscientiousness:

- Meet commitments and keep promises.
- Hold themselves accountable for meeting their objectives.
- Are organized and careful in their work.

Adaptability and innovation

People with the competency of innovation:

- Seek out fresh ideas from a wide variety of sources.
- Entertain original solutions to problems.
- Generate new ideas.
- Take fresh perspectives and risks in their thinking.

People with the competency of adaptability:

- Smoothly handle multiple demands, shifting priorities and rapid change.
- Adapt their responses and tactics to fit fluid circumstances.
- Are flexible in how they see events.

In their words

Taya's story

A month before Christmas, the company implemented a new customer relationship management (CRM) system. It was leading edge technology, and it was going to vastly improve the customer experience. In retrospect, the implementation should have happened earlier to give us more time to get used to it, but that's what happens.

Of course, as Christmas got closer, the contact volumes increased. The number of emails and telephone calls increased drastically with customers chasing orders, querying delivery dates, and changing requirements and so on. The buzz of activity felt like a deluge. The cacophony was overwhelming.

I was feeling so much pressure in trying to keep up with the volumes and navigate around the new CRM. I was feeling anxious and stressed. I observed physical manifestation of my emotions. My stomach was churning and my heart rate increased.

I called on the Regulator. I needed a mental pause to ground myself and focus on my emotions before they overwhelmed me. When my break times came around, rather than dwelling on the situation and allowing it to consume me, I went for a walk. I paid attention to my emotions and recognized that my strong reaction was not so much my inability to do my job but my distraction from it by what was happening around me. I needed to be focused on what I had to accomplish and not be distracted.

My emotional awareness, self-assessment and self-control gave me the ability to regulate what was happening and remove my anxiety and stress. There was still pressure to manage the volume of work, but I was able to keep calm and carry on.

 **Actions**

Self-awareness

Emotional awareness

In a world of constant and relentless change, our minds are preoccupied by a stream of thought: planning the next thing, immersed in the present and preoccupied with things not completed.

We need to take a mental pause and be sensitive to the underlying murmur of mood—something we rarely do. Our feelings are always

with us but we are not always with them. We typically only become aware of our feelings when they build up and boil over. However, if we pay attention, we can recognize them before they become so strong.

Meditate. Take time out to do nothing. Reserve time every week for solitary reflection. This may take the form of going for a long walk or working on a hobby.

Slow down. When you recognize that you are reacting strongly to a situation, slow down to understand why. Through increased self-awareness, you can choose how you respond rather than react.

Accurate self-assessment

Ask co-workers for feedback. This includes subordinates, peers and superiors. Seek it out on a regular basis. Ask for honest and constructive feedback about how you are doing.

Identify weaknesses and shortcomings, and work to overcome them. Know where you need to improve or learn from someone who demonstrates a skill you lack.

Be prepared to learn from mistakes and openly acknowledge them when they happen.

Self-confidence

Visualize yourself as you want to be. Visualize the fantastic *you* achieving your goals.

Practice self-affirmation. State out loud the things at which you are good.

Get outside of your comfort zone. If there is a situation in which you do not feel confident, put yourself in that situation and confront your fears. Do this on a regular basis.

When you achieve something, congratulate yourself and give yourself a pat on the back.

Set yourself goals that might stretch you but make sure they are also achievable.

Practice being assertive, saying 'no' and gaining more control over your life.

Self-regulation

Self-control

Keep focused on what needs to be done. Do not get distracted by seemingly urgent but actually trivial matters. Avoid unnecessary distractions.

Find a relaxation technique that suits you such as a simple meditation practice. Put it into daily use, perhaps allowing yourself 30 minutes of inner calm each morning before starting work.

Find a stress management technique that suits you such as sitting in a long bath, going for a long walk, a workout at the gym or a yoga session.

When experiencing emotions such as anger or hostility, keep a journal for five days. Spend 20 minutes each day writing out your deepest feelings and reflections. Monitoring emotions in this way speeds up the recovery from the distress.

Stay calm and carry on.

Develop hardiness. This is the ability to stay committed, feel in control and be challenged rather than be threatened by stress. Practice seeing work as strenuous but also exciting, and change as a chance to develop, rather than the enemy.

Trustworthiness and conscientiousness

Let people know your values and principles, and intentions and feelings and act in ways that are reliably consistent with them. Stay in alignment with your values.

Have courage and stand-up for your values.

Be forthright about your own mistakes.

Be frank and acknowledge your feelings—be authentic.

Act openly, honestly and consistently.

Practice self-restraint and think through the potential consequences of what you are about to do; assume responsibility for your words and actions.

Be careful in doing work and get things done.

Keep things running as they should.

Show concern for the people with whom you work. Assist with orientation for new starters and assimilation for those returning to work after a break.

Adaptability and innovation

Be flexible. Take in new, even painful, information without tuning out in self-protection, and respond nimbly.

Listen to customers and colleagues.

Think through all the positive scenarios related to a change. Discuss them with colleagues.

Relish change and seek exhilaration in innovation.

Be open to new information; let go of old assumptions and adapt.

Be comfortable with the anxiety that the new or unknown can bring, and be willing to take a gamble on a new way of doing things.

Be comfortable with ambiguity and remaining calm in the face of the unexpected.

Be flexible to take into account multiple perspectives on a given situation.

Be open to change.

Be creative on the job, and apply new ideas to achieve new results.

Quickly identify key issues, and simplify problems that seem overwhelmingly complex.

Find original connections and patterns that others often overlook.

Be comfortable with risk.

Form coalitions and collaborations to bring ideas to fruition.

Adapt deftly to shifting market realities through a collective creativity, and be comfortable with uncertainty.

 Reading

Emotional Intelligence: Why It Can Matter More Than IQ by Daniel Goleman

Working With Emotional Intelligence by Daniel Goleman

Emotional Intelligence 2.0 by Travis Bradberry and Jean Greaves

Go Suck a Lemon: Strategies for Improving Your Emotional Intelligence by Michael Cornwall

Links

Daniel Goleman: http://www.danielgoleman.info

The Empathizer

Superpower: Empathy

Note: Some content within this module has been reproduced from Working With Emotional Intelligence *with permission from author Daniel Goleman.*

Empathy is a dimension of emotional intelligence as explained in Daniel Goleman's book *Working with Emotional Intelligence.*

He describes empathy as the awareness of others' feelings, needs and concerns.

The empathy dimension consists of five competencies:

- **Understanding others:** Sensing others' feelings and perspectives, and taking an active interest in their concerns.
- **Developing others:** Sensing others' developmental needs and bolstering their abilities.
- **Service orientation:** Anticipating, recognizing and meeting customer needs.
- **Leveraging diversity:** Cultivating opportunities through different kinds of people.
- **Political awareness:** Reading a group's emotional currents and power relationships.

Understanding others

People with this competency:

- Are attentive to emotional cues and listen well.
- Show sensitivity and understand others' perspectives.
- Help out based on understanding other people's needs and feelings.

A finely tuned ear is key and at the heart of empathy. Listening is essential for success in the workplace. If you do not listen, you will appear to be indifferent or uncaring. This, in turn, will make others less communicative.

Developing others

People with this competency:

- Acknowledge and reward people's strengths and accomplishments.
- Offer useful feedback and identify people's needs for further growth.
- Mentor, give timely coaching, and offer projects that challenge and foster a person's skills.

Coaching is at the heart of developing others. The heart of coaching and developing is the act of counseling. The effectiveness of counseling

relies on empathy and the ability to focus on our own feelings and share them.

The best coaches show a genuine personal interest in those they seek to guide; they understand and have empathy for them. Trust is crucial.

Service orientation

People with this competency:

- Understand customers' needs and match them to services or products.
- Seek ways to increase customer satisfaction and loyalty.
- Gladly offer appropriate assistance.
- Grasp a customer's perspective, and act as a trusted advisor.

The highest level of customer service means being able to identify customer's underlying—and often unstated—needs, and matching them to one's products or services. It also means taking a long-term perspective and, therefore, sometimes trading off immediate gains in order to protect and preserve the relationship.

Superb customer service entails becoming a trusted advisor. This trust-based relationship is one that can only grow over time.

Remember, we all have customers. Any colleague we need to help or whom our actions affect is a customer. To excel at customer service, we need to monitor the satisfaction of the customer and not wait to hear complaints.

Leveraging diversity

People with this competency:

- Respect and relate well to people from varied backgrounds.
- Understand diverse world views and are sensitive to group differences.

- See diversity as opportunity; they create an environment where diverse people can thrive.
- Challenge bias and intolerance.

We should not call attention to someone's group affiliation when that identity is irrelevant. This can invoke a stereotype about that group in the minds of all concerned. Group stereotypes can have an emotional power that negatively affects performance.

To be successful in the workplace, people need to feel they belong, that they are accepted and valued, and that they have the skills and inner resources needed to achieve and prosper. When negative stereotypes undermine these assumptions, they hamper performance.

There is strength in difference and this makes the ability to leverage diversity an increasingly crucial competence.

Leveraging diversity can bring heightened profitability, enhanced organizational learning, flexibility and rapid adaptation to shifting markets.

Political awareness

People with this competency:

- Accurately read key power relationships.
- Detect crucial social networks.
- Understand the forces that shape views and actions of clients, customers or competitors.
- Accurately read organizational and external realities.

The ability to read political realities is vital to the behind-the-scenes networking and coalition building that allows you to exercise influence—no matter what your professional role.

Every organization has its own invisible nervous system of connection and influence. Some people are oblivious to it while others have it fully on their radar.

This competence of political awareness builds on both emotional self-control and empathy; it allows people to see clearly rather than be swayed by their own point of view.

In their words

Charlie's story

I had recently been promoted to team leader, and I noticed that one of my junior staff appeared to be struggling with some of the tasks she had to undertake.

I wasn't sure what was going on but I knew that I had to find out. I called on the Empathizer. I had to make sure Susan knew that I was open to listening and that I listened well.

I found a quiet space and asked Susan to join me. I enquired about her well-being and how the job was going. She started to tell me that she was extremely frustrated and stressed.

I looked for emotional cues; I encouraged Susan to keep sharing and responded with empathy. I showed understanding from her perspective. I was careful to validate my understanding of what Susan was expressing by playing back to her what she said to me. I said things like "So Susan, let me check that I understand... You are feeling..."

It soon emerged that Susan's frustration was due to Johnny (who had been assigned as her buddy) who had not shown her how to use the order fulfilment system. He was saying things like "Figure it out, that's what you're paid to do."

I made an appropriate change and found Susan a more suitable buddy.

I then had to focus on developing Johnny. Showing Johnny empathy uncovered the fact that he didn't feel confident in

showing Susan the system as he felt that he would be exposed as incompetent if he did so.

I provided Johnny with feedback on his lack of empathy for Susan's situation but also put in place a coaching program for him that would both increase his confidence and develop his empathy skills.

The result of calling on the Empathizer superpower was a much happier, cohesive, connected and collaborative team.

 # Actions

Understanding others

Establish the ability to pick up emotional cues and adjust your behavior accordingly.

Be a good communicator. Set expectations, get feedback and check understanding. Encourage conversation and listen carefully.

Empathize with customers so you can determine their needs. Get out and talk to them. Listen, feel and sense.

Demonstrate that you are open to listening. Have an open door; appear approachable and go out of your way to hear what others have to say.

Practice "active" listening. Listen well and deeply. Go beyond what is said by asking questions and restating, in your own words, what you have heard to be sure that you understand.

Demonstrate that you have truly heard someone by responding appropriately even if this means making some change in what you do.

Don't use empathy for manipulation. Empathy has to have integrity.

Developing others

Develop coaching and mentoring skills to help others perform better.

Provide feedback and offer advice on developing the skills needed.

Show a genuine interest in those you guide and have empathy and understanding for them.

Demonstrate respect and trustworthiness.

Give a consistent stream of positive and constructive performance feedback. Show belief in the ability for others to change.

Let others take the lead in setting their own goals.

Point to problems without offering solutions; this implies that you believe the other person can find the solution themselves.

Service orientation

Be prepared to forego immediate gains in order to establish, maintain, sustain and retain a customer relationship.

Take a broader view and consider your colleagues as your customers.

Be proactive and actively seek feedback to determine customer satisfaction levels. Always seek to improve customer satisfaction and take positive action to do so.

Leveraging diversity

Have zero tolerance for intolerance.

Build the three skills needed to leverage diversity:

- Get along well with people who are different.
- Appreciate the unique ways others may operate or approach a situation.

- Seize whatever business opportunities these unique approaches may offer.

Political awareness

Always be aware of what is going on around you.

Empathize on an organizational level, not just an interpersonal one, to read the currents that influence the real decision-makers.

Maintain rich personal networks in your organization and be savvy about what is going on.

Observe events objectively. Try and distance yourself, and set aside your own emotional involvement in events.

 ## Reading

Wired to Care: How Companies Prosper When They Create Widespread Empathy by Dev Patnaik

Working With Emotional Intelligence by Daniel Goleman

Empathy (HBR Emotional Intelligence Series)

Links

Daniel Goleman: http://www.danielgoleman.info

TED Talk: Why aren't we more compassionate by Daniel Goleman
https://www.ted.com/talks/daniel_goleman_why_aren_t_
we_more_compassionate?utm_campaign=tedspread&utm_
medium=referral&utm_source=tedcomshare

The Collaborator

Superpower: Collaboration

Collaboration is when two individuals or a group of people work toward achieving a common goal by sharing their ideas and skills.

It can happen in co-located teams or in geographically dispersed teams through collaboration tools and platforms.

Collaboration means shared learning, breaking down of silos, better problem-solving and being able to see the bigger picture.

When responding to constant change "nobody's as smart as everybody" because the organization must consistently identify the best way to respond to change, innovate, experiment and create.

Collaboration is the epitome of the idiom "a problem shared is a problem halved." Collaboration reduces stress and increases resilience in yourself and those with whom you collaborate. It pulls on diverse and different thinking.

Reaching out to others allows you to collaborate on the achievement of a common goal by thinking, brainstorming, and pulling on differing perspectives.

Working toward a common goal can provide inspiration and a sense of purpose. Collaboration gives you and others involved an equal opportunity to participate and share ideas.

An important element of building resilience is being prepared to ask for help. It is not a sign of weakness; it is a sign of strength.

So what do you need to do to effectively collaborate in the workplace?

Reach out

First, reach out to others. Don't wait for others to come to you. Lead by example. Reach out to others who you know will have different views to you so you can get a diversity of perspectives. This often goes against the grain as we generally like to associate with people who are like ourselves; however, diversity is critical to effective collaboration.

Clear purpose

Collaborators located together or geographically dispersed need a common and shared goal.

Team structure

Your team structure and composition will vary depending on what you are trying to achieve. If there is a specific problem you are trying to resolve, you will most likely use "closed collaboration", where you select subject matter experts to form the collaborative team. Closed collaboration may consist of a small number of collaborators—two or more people.

If you want to generate ideas and tackle big issues, you may use "open collaboration", where you invite collaborators from inside and outside the organization to get involved. This group will be larger than the closed collaboration group as you are putting out a general invitation to which anyone can respond. The advantage is that you also get a diverse range of ideas, opinions and expertise.

Platform

If the collaborators are geographically dispersed, they will need a collaboration platform. If your organization already has one, look to use that. Platforms that exist include (but are not limited to) Yammer, Slack, SharePoint, and Jive.

When people are working remotely, try and utilize video calls over telephone calls as much as possible, as the ability to read body language is of utmost importance. It allows for the creation of rapport, trust and empathy.

The right behaviors

It is imperative that the right behaviors are encouraged in order to have effective collaboration.

Collaboration excels when everyone is humble enough to accept the value that others bring. Everyone has their own strengths.

Allow others to challenge ideas and have the humility to accept the feedback. Also be humble when providing others with feedback. Do it calmly and as a considered response not a reaction.

Everyone needs to be flexible and adaptable; they must be prepared to have their mindset changed over the course of the collaboration.

When collaborating everyone should "de-label". There is no seniority or hierarchy when people truly collaborate. Everyone is equal. Everyone can contribute. Everyone has something to offer. Everyone can be heard. There is no pulling of rank over another.

Celebrate

Recognize efforts and celebrate successes. Do this publicly. Also celebrate failures as learning experiences.

In their words

Aditya's story

I have been with "the company" for some time and, therefore, know a lot of the people. It wasn't until I pulled on the Collaborator superpower that I realized the breadth and depth of knowledge they all had. I had known these people but never worked with them on anything before.

I was grappling to find the most effective way to increase financial knowledge across the organization. The aim was to raise awareness of the need to maintain a record of expenditure across all departments. Whatever solution I came up with, I could always envisage parts of the organization not embracing it.

I used the Collaborator superpower and, hey presto, we came up with a solution. We had a closed collaboration group with membership from each department. We used Slack to enable collaboration across locations and through a series of brainstorming sessions got a great outcome.

Collaboration made me feel so resilient knowing that I could reach out and get assistance from across the organization. I didn't have to resolve a problem all by myself.

 **Actions**

Reach out

Reach out to a diverse group of people and invite them to collaborate.

Clear purpose

Get everyone on the same page. Discuss and agree the short- and long-term goals and how you intend to collaborate to achieve them.

Team structure

Determine which team structure will work best.

Ensure you achieve a diversity of membership. Find people with different perspectives and opinions. Select people with the skills and expertise necessary to address the problem to be solved or opportunity to be exploited. Include people who are prepared to challenge assumptions and the status quo.

Have clear roles and responsibilities across the group and agree to them. You may want to consider the appointment of a facilitator for the collaboration and keep things focused on the task at hand. However, note that this person is not necessarily the "lead". Everyone should be given a chance to lead.

Platform

Determine what collaboration platforms already exist and if they can be leveraged. If no platform exists, determine other tools at your disposal and whether they can be leveraged.

Investigate available collaboration tools and make a business case for the one that suits your collaboration needs and those of the wider organization. If it is to be an organization-wide platform, this will involve other stakeholder groups.

Encourage active use of the platform. Monitor usage to determine whether action is needed to increase usage.

Right behaviors

Make sure everyone understands the behaviors needed to effectively collaborate.

Agree on the behaviors and give everyone permission to call others on their behavior if it is not positively contributing to the collaboration.

Celebrate

Determine the most appropriate way to celebrate collaboration wins. Do this on a regular basis but not at a frequency where the celebration loses relevance.

 ## Reading

Collaboration Begins With You: Be A Silo Buster by Ken Blanchard, Jane Ripley and Eunice Parisi-Carew.

Collaboration: How Leaders Avoid the Traps, Build Common Ground, and Reap Big Results by Morten Hansen

 ## Links

TED Talk: How to turn a group of strangers into a team by Amy Edmonson
https://www.ted.com/talks/amy_edmondson_how_to_turn_a_group_of_strangers_into_a_team?utm_campaign=tedspread&utm_medium=referral&utm_source=tedcomshare

The Explorer

Superpower: Exploration

The Explorer is curious and inquisitive. Exploration means always seeking out new challenges and opportunities, and being ready to navigate our volatile, uncertain, complex and ambiguous world of change while seeking out opportunities for learning, sharing and growth.

The Explorer will investigate, is eager for knowledge, and is unduly curious and inquiring. Exploration means asking questions, finding answers, looking in new places, and getting as much information as possible.

The Explorer is passionate about learning and will persevere to achieve their goals.

The Explorer has a growth mindset and sees a challenge as an opportunity to learn rather than a hurdle or threat to overcome.

The Explorer has grit and can dig deep when the going gets tough. They have the drive to sustain their motivation and ignite their passion for a long-term goal.

A growth mindset *and* grit are core to resilience.

Growth mindset

After studying the behavior of thousands of children, Carol Dweck, Ph.D., coined the terms fixed mindset and growth mindset. These mindsets describe how we view our intelligence and personality. Dweck wrote about these mindsets in her 2007 publication *Mindset: The New Psychology of Success.*

With a fixed mindset, you believe you have *finite* amounts of characteristics: intelligence, personality, morality etc. You feel the need to prove yourself in order to demonstrate that you have these characteristics—and enough of them.

With a growth mindset, you believe you have *basic* qualities and characteristics. You differ from others in regards to your inherent talents, aptitudes, interests and disposition, but with a growth mindset, you believe that you can change and grow.

Here is an example to demonstrate the difference between a fixed and growth mindset:

It's performance review time with your boss. Upon reflection, you believe you did really well; however, your boss doesn't have the same opinion and believes you have areas for self-development. You are upset.

On the way home from work, you get a flat tire and have to call for roadside assistance, which takes forever to arrive and means you arrive home late.

When you get home, you call one of your siblings to discuss your day and your frustration but you feel you are being given the cold shoulder, which makes your day worse.

You can consider the events of your day in two ways.

With a fixed mindset, you are likely to tell yourself:

- I'm a failure.
- I'm stupid.
- I'm going nowhere.
- I'm on my own.
- No-one cares.

With a growth mindset, you are likely to tell yourself:

- I need to follow the advice of my boss and work harder in some areas of my development.
- I need to get my car serviced more often and get my wheels aligned.
- I need to learn how to change a tire myself and check my spare tire is in good condition.
- I wonder if my sibling also had a bad day; maybe worse than mine.

So, given that the majority of us would like to operate with a growth mindset: what would be your coping strategies in the above situation?

You could start by:

- Working harder on professional development or finding alternative ways of working toward a goal.
- Putting in place a development plan.
- Calling your sibling to check they are okay.
- Schedule time to learn basic car maintenance skills.

People with a growth mindset don't throw their hands up in despair. They can get just as upset or frustrated as those with a fixed mindset, but they choose to meet the challenges head on, work at overcoming them, and invest in personal development and growth.

A fixed mindset is about validation. A growth mindset is about development.

You have a choice: just as you can change your mind, you can change your beliefs. You can either believe that your intellect and abilities are static or believe that they can evolve and grow.

The weaknesses of a fixed mindset

People with a fixed mindset:

- Rarely shine
- Give up after a couple of failures
- Are humiliated by failure
- Avoid challenges
- Believe that putting in the effort to learn is pointless
- Are threatened by the success of others
- Are envious of the success of others.

The supremacies of a growth mindset

People with a growth mindset:

- Shine
- Believe that hard work and commitment enable growth
- Want to learn
- Embrace challenges
- Persevere
- Are resilient
- Are inspired by the success of others
- Embrace hard work and effort
- Learn from the success of others
- Continually grow
- Succeed

- Achieve
- Are more productive
- Have better relationships.

Grit

Angela Duckworth, in her book *Grit: The Power of Passion and Perseverance*, describes grit as having passion and perseverance to achieve long-term and meaningful goals, and that with grit comes resilience.

Duckworth is a University of Pennsylvania psychologist, and her study of grit began when she was teaching math to 12- and 13-year-olds. She recognized that IQ (talent) was not the only factor separating successful students from those who were struggling, and that grit was the combination of perseverance and passion for the achievement of long-term goals.

She went on to research the short- and long-term effects of grit on students and people at work. So, although the study of grit originated in education, the principles apply in the workplace too.

Duckworth's research revealed four psychological assets whom exemplars of grit possess. They develop over the years in a particular order. They are interest, practice, purpose and hope.

Interest is about enjoying what you do. We all have aspects of our work that we don't enjoy. When we have grit, we can see our work as the whole of many parts and find it meaningful and interesting. People with grit love what they do.

Practice is about perseverance and the daily self-control to do something better than you did it yesterday. With grit, you strive for mastery through regular and sustained practice. You identify your areas of weakness and work to improve them. There is no room for complacency. Practice is about devotion to improvement and embracing challenges.

Purpose is what matures passion. Purpose is the belief that your work matters not just for you, but for others. Without having a purpose, any interest will be difficult to sustain.

Hope is not the last stage of grit but it is in every stage of grit. We have to be able to keep going and face our doubts and demons. We will get knocked down but we can't stay down. If we stay down, we lose. When we get up, we prevail.

In their words

Maria's story

I didn't even know I had superpowers until I was introduced to the Resiliator.

One of my superpowers is the Explorer. I don't know whether it is nature or nurture but I have always been determined to learn more and develop myself. I also have persistence and perseverance to master something. I called it stubbornness but now I call it the Explorer superpower.

It makes me more resilient, as I am prepared to have a go, and if something doesn't work, I will adapt and flex until it does. I will keep trying despite setbacks. Sometimes that is hard, and there are times when I get knocked down and don't feel like getting back up again. But I believe I have a choice. I can stay down or get up and keep going. I think the latter is a better option.

I have called on the Explorer both at work and at home. At home, I persisted in learning to play the banjo. I believed I could do it but also knew that it wouldn't happen overnight. I persevered and now I am pretty good.

In regards to work, a big gap in my marketing capability was data analytics. I am great with words but not so good with numbers. In fact, I loathe them. I knew that I would not further my marketing

career if I did not master data analytics. I had a growth mindset and put in the time and effort needed to learn and develop. Despite my uptake being slower than I would have liked at times, I persevered. I now have a senior marketing role as a result.

 **Actions**

Growth mindset

Read Dweck's book *Mindset: The New Psychology of Success*

Test your mindset to discover if you have a fixed or growth mindset. Try this interactive quiz from the London Academy of IT. https://www.londonacademyofit.co.uk/blog/interactive-quiz-fixed-vs-growth-mindset"

Change your mindset using the following steps:

1. **Understand it**

   Understand how the brain works. The brain is a muscle and the more you practice the stronger that muscle becomes. In 1998, scientists discovered that the brain is plastic (neuroplasticity), and that it changes constantly throughout its life. When we think, act, learn and develop, the brain's anatomy changes accordingly—it grows new brain cells. So the bottom line is "use it or lose it."

2. **Recognize it**

   Recognize when you have a fixed mindset about something.

   When you face a challenge, the inner voice of a fixed mindset will say, "Are you sure you can do this?" "What if you fail?" "People will laugh at you." "Don't do it and save face."

When you have a setback, the inner voice of a fixed mindset will say, "I told you so."

When you face criticism, the inner voice of a fixed mindset will say, "Who do they think they are?"

3. Change it

Recognize that you can change it. You have a choice. You can keep the fixed mindset and the perils it brings or you can interpret the setbacks, criticism and challenges with a growth mindset. You can see them as signs that you can improve and develop. You can embrace the challenge, propel yourself toward new goals, and rise to the top.

4. Talk to it

When you hear your fixed mindset saying, "You will fail," retort with "The most successful people have had failures."

When you hear your fixed mindset saying, "I don't want to fail," retort with "I will learn through failure and be stronger for it."

When you hear your fixed mindset saying, "It wasn't my fault," retort with "I can only fix it if I take responsibility for it."

When you hear your fixed mindset saying, "If I had the talent this would have been a breeze," retort with "That is so wrong. Soccer wasn't easy for Ronaldo. Writing wasn't easy to J.K. Rowling. They both had passion and put in the hard work and effort."

When you hear your fixed mindset saying, "I can't do it," retort with "I can't do it *now* but I can learn to do it with time and hard work."

5. Act on it

When you hear the fixed mindset talking, you can respond with a growth mindset and determine the actions you need to take to learn and grow.

You can view failure as a learning opportunity.

You can acknowledge your skills and talents.

You can ask others for feedback so you can identify areas for growth.

You can see challenges as opportunities rather than problems.

You can become curious and develop an appetite for learning.

You can choose not to focus on what happened to you but on what is happening to you.

You can recognize that setbacks are temporary and there is another way to get to where you want to go.

You can celebrate the successes of others. Reap what you sow.

You can practice. Moving from a fixed mindset to a growth mindset will take practice.

You can keep on setting goals for growth. Keep seeking out opportunities for learning and development.

You can maintain and continue the growth.

Grit

Read Duckworth's book *Grit: The Power of Passion and Perseverance*

Use the Grit Scale to discover your level of passion and perseverance. https://angeladuckworth.com/grit-scale/

Interest

1. Seek activities that interest you at work. What are you passionate about?

2. Get out there and discover what excites you.

3. Determine how best you could turn that passion into capability. This could be finding an opportunity to take on a role that allows you to use that passion and develop it into a skill. It could be seeking out a coach or mentor to assist you in leveraging your passion.

Practice

1. You need to practice. Hard work develops skill.

2. Identify weaknesses and work to improve them. Remember that practice takes time.

3. Have fun. Turn practice into a game or challenge. Aim to be better than the person you were yesterday.

4. Deliberate practice means you are learning along the way. Practice is not about repetition, it is about doing things differently. If you are just repeating the same thing over and over, you are not improving. Repetition is not expertise.

5. Get feedback from your experience as well as from others.

Purpose

1. The difference between someone who is just working hard and someone who has real grit is that the latter finds meaning in what they do.

2. Find purpose in what you are doing. It is about how important your actions are to you *and* others.

3. If you have grit, you don't just have a "job," you have a "calling." Love what you do.

Hope

1. Believe things will improve because it is you who will improve them.

2. Have a growth mindset and be a realistic optimist. See the Realistic Optimist.

3. Bounce back in the face of adversity. Persevere. There are no limits.

4. Have self-belief. Say, "I can." Now say it again.

5. Spend time with other 'gritty' people.

 # Reading

Mindset: The New Psychology of Success by Carol S. Dweck

Grit: The Power of Passions and Perseverance by Angela Duckworth

Leading With Grit: Inspiring Action and Accountability With Generosity, Respect, Integrity, and Truth by Laurie Sudbrink

Links

Angela Duckworth: https://angeladuckworth.com

Grit Scale: https://angeladuckworth.com/grit-scale/

TED Talk: The power of believing that you can improve by Carol Dweck https://www.ted.com/talks/carol_dweck_the_power_of_believing_that_you_can_improve?utm_campaign=tedspread&utm_medium=referral&utm_source=tedcomshare

TED Talk Grit: The power of passion and perseverance by Angela Duckworth https://www.ted.com/talks/angela_lee_duckworth_grit_the_power_of_passion_and_perseverance?utm_campaign=tedspread&utm_medium=referral&utm_source=tedcomshare

The Experimenter

Superpower: Experimentation

The Experimenter tries new things. Resilience means being adventurous. It means being prepared to experiment, embracing the vulnerability that this brings, accepting that there will be mistakes and recovering from failure. It is okay to jump into the unknown. It is okay to take risks.

Innovation is now key to organizational survival and innovation is fueled from experimentation. You cannot change things for the better if you are not prepared to experiment. Be prepared to fail along the way. Failure is a way of learning what doesn't work and what does. If you accept failure, you will lack resilience.

There are endless stories of innovation failures from organizations and people who are extremely successful. They are successful because they were prepared to experiment. Examples of failure include Apple III, Google Wave and Microsoft Zune but yet these organizations thrive.

3M experimented with glue, which was a failure because it didn't stick, but that failure led to the basis for the Post-it™, which is a huge success.

Recognizing failure as a learning process has led to the word "fail" being used as acronyms for learning and resilience. These include:

- First Action in Learning
- First Attempt at Learning
- Forever Acquiring Important Lessons
- Found Another Interesting Lesson
- Future Always Involves Learning.

Where do experiments come from?

Sometimes we forget to think outside the square and continue to do things the way they have always been done.

Look at things from a different perspective. Take a walk in someone else's shoes. It could be a customer, consumer or colleague. Have a look at how their experience could be improved.

Have a look around and identify things that feel broken. How could you fix them? What could you change?

Share thoughts with others and gather their feedback. This could lead to different and better ideas.

Extend your view of the world and gather ideas through reading, browsing the Internet and looking at sources of information that you wouldn't usually reference.

In their words

Charlie's story

I was very excited when I was given the team leader position. I knew the team was not a cohesive bunch, and I wanted to

improve its collaboration and communication. I wanted to think outside the square and experiment rather than send the team on a communication course or offer online learning.

I wanted experimentation to encourage creativity and innovation.

I wanted to drive change with them and not to them. So I tried an experiment. I encouraged every member of the team to identify a trait, within the team, that they would like to change. Then they were to find a team building exercise (time boxed duration) to facilitate improvement.

I communicated the purpose of the exercise with clarity and ensured we were all on the same page. I also made it clear that this was an experiment and that some of the team building exercises may be a success while others may fail. I explained that this was okay, and that we would learn from the successes as well as the failures.

At the start of each team meeting, a new team building exercise was tried. The team had great fun and became better communicators and collaborators as a result. Everyone became more resilient as they learnt to lean on each other when needed.

Actions

Determine the experiment that you would like to try. Depending on the nature of the experiment and your position within your organization, you may need to seek out permission to conduct it.

Test out your ideas with customers, consumers and colleagues before commencing.

Create a hypothesis: your prediction for what will happen if the experiment is successful.

When designing the experiment, cover what you are going to test and for how long. Include control groups and measurements.

Run the experiment, incorporating communication, to impacted parties and stakeholders. Monitor the experiment and ensure that nothing takes place that could interfere with the results, for example, other organizational changes. You may have to rerun the experiment if interference happens.

Analyze the results and compare them with your expectations and hypothesis.

Determine how you can use what you have learned. Do you need to do more experiments or can you take action on what you have learned?

Celebrate success as well as failure.

Reading

What's the Big Idea? Creating and Capitalizing on the Best Management Thinking by Thomas H. Davenport

Fail More: Embrace, Learn, and Adapt to Failure as a Way to Success by Bill Wooditch

Links

TED Talk: Creating a Culture of Rapid Experimentation by Kaaren Hanson - https://youtu.be/7-WLX8gc8WY

The Solver

Superpower: Problem-solving

The ability to effectively solve problems is key to being resilient. The way in which you consider and approach problems helps you build resilience.

Like other Resiliator superpowers, problem-solving can be learned.

There are many approaches to problem-solving and we will explore some here. Whichever approach best suits your problem-solving, remember that a collaborative approach is generally most beneficial.

Einstein, one of the most famous scientists and problem-solvers in history, is often heralded as a lone figure working in obscurity. However, history has also shown that this was *not* the situation and that Einstein frequently shared and explored his ideas with friends and colleagues.

He referred to one of these colleagues Michele Besso, as "the best sounding board in Europe."

So, even the greatest problem-solvers collaborate. The Solver leverages basic problem-solving, creative problem-solving and design thinking among other problem-solving approaches.

Basic problem-solving

1. **Define the problem:** Clearly identify the problem. What issue is it causing? What are the disclosing signs that it is a problem? You may want to break down the problem into smaller parts if the problem, as a whole, seems overbearing. This is the most important step because if you don't fully understand the problem, the subsequent steps could be irrelevant to finding a solution.

2. **Generate solutions:** Generate as many solutions as possible. This is like brainstorming. The aim is not to be overly critical or judgmental of the proposed solutions but to be as creative as possible.

3. **Evaluate options:** All of the options should be evaluated and the best one chosen for implementation. Sometimes, this may not be an exact science but more of a gut feeling.

4. **Implement and monitor:** Implement the selected solution and monitor the situation to determine if the problem has been resolved. If the solution has not resolved the problem, return to step 1.

Solutions should be generated using a combination of creative, analytical and practical problem-solving styles.

Creative problem-solving

Creative problem-solving (CPS) is a process formulated by Alex Osborn and Sidney Parnes in the 1940s and 1950s.

The Creative Education Foundation[10] has a four-stage CPS model with a total of six explicit process steps. Each step uses divergent and convergent thinking. It is called the CPS Learner's Model.[11]

The following has been reproduced with the permission of the Creative Education Foundation.[12]

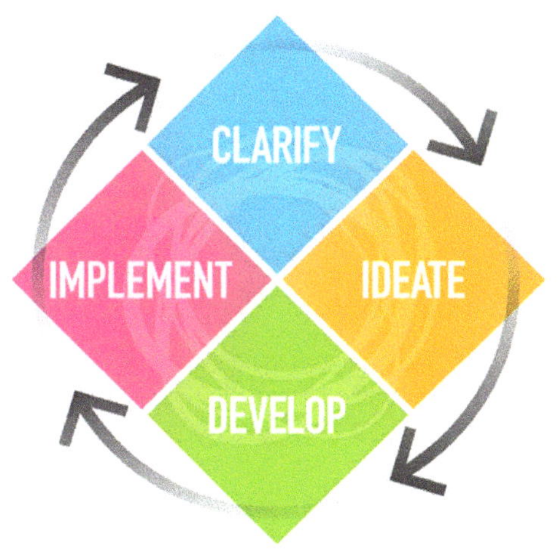

Stage	Step	Purpose
CLARIFY	*Explore the vision*	Identify the goal, wish or challenge.
	Gather data	Describe and generate data to enable a clear understanding of the challenge.
	Formulate challenges	Sharpen awareness of the challenge and create challenge questions that invite solutions.
IDEATE	*Explore ideas*	Generate ideas that answer the challenge questions.
DEVELOP	*Formulate solutions*	To move from ideas to solutions, evaluate, strengthen, and select solutions for best "fit."
IMPLEMENT	*Formulate a plan*	Explore acceptance and identify resources and actions that will support implementation of the selected solution(s).

CPS begins with two assumptions:

- Everyone is creative in some way.
- Creative skills can be learned and enhanced.

The core principles are:

1. **Divergent and convergent thinking must be balanced:** Keys to creativity are learning ways to identify and balance expanding and contracting thinking (done separately), and knowing when to practice them.

2. **Ask problems as questions:** Solutions are more readily invited and developed when challenges and problems are restated as open-ended questions with multiple possibilities. Such questions generate lots of rich information, while closed-ended questions tend to elicit confirmation or denial. Statements tend to generate limited or no response at all.

3. **Defer or suspend judgment:** As Osborn learned in his early work on brainstorming, the instantaneous judgment in response to an idea shuts down idea generation. There is an appropriate and necessary time to apply judgment when converging.

4. **Focus on "Yes, and" rather than "No, but":** When generating information and ideas, language matters. "Yes, and" allows continuation and expansion, which is necessary in certain stages of CPS. The use of the word "but"—preceded by "yes" or "no"— closes down conversation, negating everything that has come before it.

Design thinking

Design thinking is another approach for creative problem-solving. It is a solution-based approach and uses analytical, synthetic, divergent and convergent thinking to create a wide number of potential solutions. These solutions are narrowed down to a "best fit" solution.

There are many versions of design thinking in use today. I will focus on the five-phase model proposed by the Hasso Plattner Institute of

Design at Stanford, which is also known as d.school. I have chosen d.school's approach because it's at the forefront of applying and teaching, design thinking.

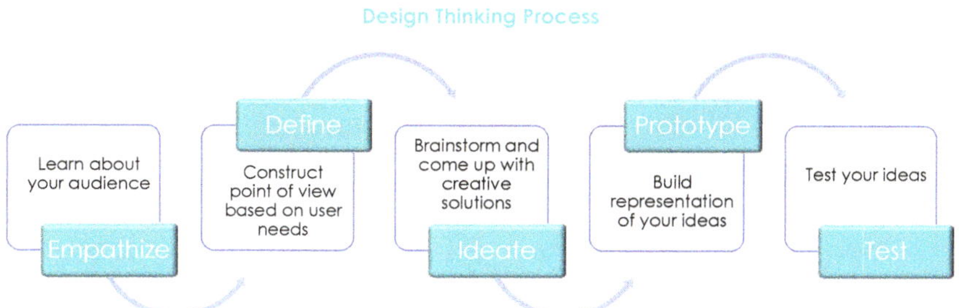

According to d.school, there are five phases of design thinking. These are:

- **Empathize.** Empathize with your audience—your customers, consumers or colleagues. Immerse yourself in their experience. Observe, engage and empathize to understand their experience and needs. You need to set aside your own perspectives and assumptions in order to gain true insight.

- **Define.** Using the information gained in the "empathize" phase, you can define the audience's needs, problems and insights. The problem statement should be human-centric. Rather than it being organizationally focused: "How do we get more students to open savings accounts?" Make it human-centric focused: "How can we create a financial safety net for students?"

- **Ideate.** Having completed phases 1 and 2, you can start to ideate. Think outside the box and generate new ideas to resolve the problem. Look at it from many perspectives. Ideation can be carried out using techniques like brainstorming, the Worst Possible Idea, and SCAMPER (Substitute, Combine, Adapt, Modify, Put to another user, Eliminate and Reverse).

- **Prototype.** This is where you (and the team) start to generate solutions. Prototypes of products or services are created. This is an experimental phase and each of the solutions is applied to the prototypes. The solutions can be tested in or outside the team

or both. Each solution is examined to determine whether it is accepted or rejected based on the audience's experience.

5. **Test.** This is the final stage but it is iterative. The team will test the solutions identified in the prototype phase to work out which best addresses the problem and the audience's experience. Even as each test takes place, alterations and refinements can be made to deliver a better solution. This process continues until you are satisfied with the outcome.

It is important to note that the five phases are not always sequential. They do not have to follow a specific order and can often occur in parallel.

In their words

Taya's story

My manager in the contact center asked if I could help some of my colleagues determine why the first contact resolution rates where much better on some teams than others.

I had no idea where to start, so I called on the Solver superpower. As a team, it was decided that creative problem-solving would be the technique to try. At this point, no one had any sense of what the problem could be.

We consulted the Creative Education Foundation and other problem-solving resources to obtain as much guidance as we could.

Using the "clarify, ideate, develop and implement" approach, we were able to produce a plan that presented implementation options for the solutions we had identified.

The problem turned out to be a technical issue with the knowledge base that was not presenting resolution options under certain conditions. It was easily resolved.

The team learned a lot about problem-solving and we were more resilient, as a result, knowing that we could repeat the exercise to keep improving our environment.

Actions

Identify and define your problem.

Decide which problem-solving technique is best suited to the situation.

Undertake research on alternative problem-solving techniques.

Share your findings with others in your organization.

Reading

Problem Solving 101: A Simple Book for Smart People by Ken Watanabe

Stop Guessing: The 9 Behaviors of Great Problem Solvers by Nat Greene

Strategies for Creative Problem-Solving by H. Scott Fogler, Steven E. LeBlanc, Benjamin Rizzo

This Is Service Design Doing: Applying Service Design Thinking in the Real World by Marc Stickdorn, Markus Edgar Hormess, Adam Lawrence and Jakob Schneider

Links

Creative Education Foundation
http://www.creativeeducationfoundation.org/creative-problem-solving/the-cps-process/

Stanford D School
https://dschool.stanford.edu

The Categorizer

Superpower: Categorization

The Categorizer uses categorization and compartmentalization to enable focus and build resilience.

Research has found that the body sends 11 million bits of information to the brain for processing every second.[13] The brain, however, can only deal with around 50 bits per second. We cannot change the number of bits sent to the brain, but we can decide what to focus on.

Stress comes from not being able to categorize, prioritize or focus on what is important. It also comes from hopping from one thing to the other and back again without taking the time to get one job done at a time.

If you cannot categorize and compartmentalize, you will not be resilient in the face of constant change. Instead, you will be continually

distracted and stressed. You will be thinking of the emails you need to answer while also planning the next team meeting, the next project meeting, and the next report you have to write. None of them will be done effectively as each is distracting from the other.

When you categorize work, you focus on one thing at a time. Think of your mind as a set of folders. Put each thing that needs to be done into its folder. Prioritize the work and pull out the appropriate folder when you need to deal with it.

The art of categorization is even more important now that we are connected 24/7. Work life can interfere with home life and vice versa. This is why categorization and prioritization is important; it helps to avoid either life from suffering.

I recognize that we may categorize our work and allocate a particular time to "writing that report." Then, despite best intentions, that time gets interrupted by a colleague who wants to pick your brain. You can choose how to deal with the interruption. You can arrange to have the conversation at a later time or decide to accept the interruption as you reckon it will only take a few minutes. There is no right or wrong. It is what works best for you. But you do need to avoid constant interruption. So, when working on one of your work categories, find a place where you are less likely to be disturbed unless it is an absolute emergency. You could also allocate time to the category of 'collaboration' when your door is open for a period and people know they can come to pick your brain.

Also, when categorizing your work, ask yourself if this category is something you should be doing. The first step to effective categorization is to get rid of the work *you* shouldn't be doing and work out *who* should be doing it.

If you can't complete one category in one time allocation, that is okay. Split it into manageable chunks so you have time to complete it. If you have a deadline for a piece of work, whether self-imposed or not, work back from that deadline and allocate chunks of time to work on that category.

In their words

Aditya's story

I was feeling so stressed with the increasing number of things crossing my desk. My emails were increasing and my in-tray was piling up. Whatever I did, I didn't seem to be getting anywhere. It didn't feel like the workload was decreasing. I was treading water and getting nowhere fast.

I was going from trying to deal with one thing to trying to deal with another and getting nothing done. I was going backwards and forwards with nothing to show for it.

The Categorizer to the rescue. I wondered how I could better categorize and prioritize my work.

I came across an article that quoted Dwight D Eisenhower as saying:

> *"What is important is seldom urgent and what is urgent is seldom important."*

It referred to the Eisenhower Decision Matrix. I took the matrix and made a table like the one shown below.

At the end of each day, I would write down the things I had to do the next day. I would then categorize the list using traffic light colors.

PRIORITY	DESCRIPTION
Important and urgent	Require my immediate attention. Crisis, problem or deadline.
Important but not urgent	No deadline but important work goals. Most of my time should be spent here.
Not important but urgent	Require attention but do not help me with work goals. Mainly interruptions from other people to fulfill their goals.
Not important and not urgent	Distractions and procrastinations. Stop doing this or spend little time doing this.

I would work my way down the list and hopefully spend little or no time in the "not important and not urgent" category.

I would avoid distractions such as emails. I decided that if an email was important and urgent, I would receive a telephone call or an in-person visit to alert me to the fact. If that did not happen, the email could wait.

The outcome was amazing. Just sorting everything into the different categories with their associated priorities removed the stress I had been feeling. I felt resilient in that more change could come and I would be able to deal with it effectively by using this approach. I constantly reminded myself that busy does not equate to productive.

Actions

Create your categories. Isolate the work from all of the other work you need to undertake.

Prioritize the categories, so you know which are most important.

Determine whether dealing with the category is making the best use of your time and, if not, determine who else should be doing it. Get rid of it.

Say "no" to work that doesn't warrant a category.

Use your calendar to allocate time to a category.

Focus on a category depending on its priority and close the door behind you. Focus.

Stay focused.

Time up? Move on to the next category.

Use the Eisenhower Priority Matrix.

 # Reading

Your Brain at Work: Strategies for Overcoming Distraction, Regaining Focus, and Working Smarter All Day Long by David Rock

Smart Work: How to Boost Your Productivity in 3 Easy Steps by Dermot Crowley

Getting Things Done: The Art of Stress-Free Productivity by David Allen

 # Links

Eisenhower Priority Matrix

https://www.eisenhower.me/eisenhower-matrix/

The Observer

Superpower: Observation

The Observer practices self-observation and mindfulness.

Self-observation

Self-observation is the practice of becoming self-aware. Self-observation is key to mental well-being and increasing resilience.

In order to grow and become more resilient, you need the ability to self-observe. It is important that you regularly look at what you do, and how you do it.

When you practice self-observation, you are non-judgmental and turn your attention inward to watch your behaviors, words, emotions and attitudes. Imagine watching yourself from a distance, as a character in a movie.

By checking in on ourselves, we can make changes that allow us to be more purposeful and effective.

Breathing and focus are key to self-observation because they can help direct attention inward and quiet the mind. When you pay attention to your breathing—slowly inhaling and exhaling—your mental state becomes more receptive. As your breathing deepens, you will feel grounded; the heart opens to be more receptive to you and others.

It is important to gently return focus to your breathing when you notice you have become distracted.

Self-observation takes practice. It is often hard to check in without judgment. It is easier to begin practicing self-awareness when you are less stressed and anxious. When you are more practiced, you can apply it to more stressful situations.

Mindfulness

The Observer practices mindfulness. You can observe yourself through meditation.

The Observer is able to pause, stand back, observe and reflect. Mindfulness decreases stress and increases resilience.

We all naturally possess mindfulness but it becomes more readily available when we practice it on a regular basis.

The aim of mindfulness is to make us aware of the internal workings of our mental, emotional and physical processes.

The practice can involve sitting comfortably, focusing on your breathing, and bringing your mind's attention to the present without drifting into concerns about the past or the future. It can also be practiced at any time. You can focus on the present when walking or driving or taking a shower.

The objective is to be as fully present, in the moment, as possible. It can be summed up in three words: be here now. It facilitates disengagement from worries, upsets or concerns, and it helps regain perspective and a deeper sense of self.

The practice of mindfulness can:

- Reduce anxiety and stress
- Increase energy levels
- Create a sense of calm
- Enhance awareness and creativity
- Improve concentration and increase productivity
- Improve relationships
- Improve emotional and physical well-being.

In their words

Charlie's story

The rate of change in distribution was crazy. New systems and technologies, along with increasing home delivery and high traffic volumes, were taking their toll.

I was suffering change fatigue. I was anxious and stressed, and my energy levels where at an all-time low. I was also a new team leader, which had its own pressures and demands.

I needed to find a sense of calm. Someone suggested that I practice mindfulness.

I shrugged my shoulders thinking all that meditation stuff was for hippies and the like. It was only when I was made aware that Richmond Football Club (Australian Football League (AFL)) accredited its 2017 Premiership win, in part, to its mindfulness program, that I really took an interest.

If it worked for those guys, I am sure it could work for me.

I did some reading and I started with mindful breathing. I could do this anywhere and at any time. I then practiced mindful observation, awareness, listening, immersion and appreciation.

Despite my doubts, these exercises really helped me cope with my stress and anxiety. Through regular practice, I was able to root my mind in the present moment and deal with challenges in a clear-minded, calm and confident manner. I was a convert.

Actions

Self-observation

Focus on your breathing.

Listen to your internal voice and what it is telling you. As the observer, observe this from a distance. This can be powerful—a moment of awakening.

Accept the internal voice and don't judge. There is no right or wrong. You are just observing. As the observer, don't get drawn into the conversation or the associated emotions.

For example, don't see yourself as an angry person and think you are like that all of the time. Rather, you can observe, "I'm feeling very angry right now," or even "The anger is pretty strong right now."

Observing from a distance allows you to make choices rather than automatically reacting as you may have done previously. As the observer, try and determine if the internal voice and conversation is sourced by past experiences or perceptions of the future.

Ask questions: "What's going on? What's driving this? What else can I learn about this? What are the biases? What are the distractions? How

is my body responding? Is it relaxed or stressed? Is the internal voice positive or negative?"

Try as much as possible to continue to stand back and observe. It can be difficult to remain removed from the internal voice and not get drawn back into the conversation.

By becoming more aware of the self we are observing, we can start to make changes as needed. We can have more control over that internal voice.

Mindfulness

Mindfulness can be practiced at any time; it is all about paying attention to the present moment. You can do this when driving, walking, running, brushing your hair. The crux is to only focus on the present moment and not to think about the past or the future.

Ask yourself present questions such as:

"Is my breathing fast or slow?"

"Am I warm or cold?"

"What can I smell?"

"What can I hear?"

Don't judge. Just notice things as they are. Don't label things. A smell is not "good" or "bad." It is just a smell. Don't judge it.

You may find it easier to practice mindfulness through meditation.

Find a place free from noise and distraction. Sit comfortably. Play soothing music or white noise if it helps.

Focus on your breathing. Control your breathing. As you breathe in, count to four. Hold your breath for two counts and then count to four as you exhale.

You may find it helpful to download an app. Useful apps promoting mindfulness include (but are not limited to) Headspace, Smiling Mind, Spire, Mental Workout, Calm, Whil and Simple Habit.

 # Reading

Fully Present: The Art, Science and Practice of Mindfulness by Diana Winston and Susan Smalley

Mindfulness: An Eight-Week Plan for Finding Peace in a Frantic World by Mark Williams and Danny Penman

Self-Observation: The Awakening of Conscience: An Owner's Manual by Red Hawk

Links

TED Talk: All it takes is 10 mindful minutes by Andy Puddicombe
https://www.ted.com/talks/andy_puddicombe_all_it_takes_is_10_
mindful_minutes.htmlTED/discussion

The Questioner

Superpower: Questioning

The Questioner is curious and will challenge the status quo.

The Questioner uses their imagination and thinks outside the box as well as questioning existing ways of doing things. This aptitude to challenge the status quo and draw on a wide range of ideas helps them be resilient in a world of constant change.

When problems or challenges occur, they ask questions and encourage curiosity. Their focus on questioning leads to identification of solutions rather than a focus on the past.

You are at your best when you are a Questioner who is looking to discover new ways of working. You need to keep learning and developing. You can become a specialist in something but the rate of change will make you irrelevant unless you continue to learn.

Organizations who can adapt will survive in the face of constant change but they can only do this if everyone asks questions and are curious.

The questions they ask include:

Why are we doing it this way?

How can we do this better?

Who can help us?

Why?

Why not?

It is easy to keep on doing things in the way they have always been done. But this is short lived. When change is constant, we all need to be looking to the future and asking:

What's next?

Why don't we do this?

What if?

We need to be curious about the possibilities.

The Questioner also becomes a great connector as they discover what other people do and how their work supports that of others. Questioners and the curious provide the organization with a competitive advantage as they intensify innovation.

In their words

Aditya's story

Looking around me, at the rest of the organization, I could see many departments making fundamental changes in the way they worked and thought. Work and progress was becoming more visual, and they were talking about increased agility in everything they did.

I felt that the finance department was getting left behind. We were, after all, just dusty old accountants. I felt that we could be overtaken and become irrelevant if we didn't make some changes in line with what was happening around us. The possibility of that concerned and stressed me.

I needed to challenge the status quo. I needed the Questioner superpower.

I found a few others, in the department, who were thinking similar things. We sought out people (supporters) from other departments who had made successful changes in their ways of working and asked them to talk to the finance department.

These supporters talked to our group as whole, not as individual departments. This demonstrated that this was not an isolated change in direction but one that was having success across the entire organization.

We didn't make radical changes overnight but we learnt from these other departments and implemented small incremental changes over time. When we achieved improvements, we celebrated; this gave us the determination to do more.

The courage we found in making small changes through collaboration and communication increased our resilience. We knew that, to some degree, our destiny was in our hands and we could make a difference.

Actions

Here are some ways you can be the Questioner and foster curiosity.

Find out what 'rocks your boat'. Go exploring. Find out what interests you and what you would like to know more about. Get curious.

Think about how you could do things better. How could you approach this project differently? How could you change something that makes no sense into a learning experience?

Connect with your colleagues and ask questions about what they do and why.

Question the status quo and ask, "How I can stop the autopilot and turn on the curiosity?"

If you want to challenge the status quo:

Make sure you prioritize your ideas and focus on one or two. You may have many ideas but a stream of suggestions can dilute your influence to make things happen.

Don't go it alone. Seek out others who support your idea. Not only can your idea improve as more people contribute but it can gain position as more people support it.

Seek out a diverse group of supporters. This will demonstrate that it has widespread support across divergent groups of people.

Persevere. Challenges to the status quo don't get accepted overnight. You might need to maintain your perseverance and persistence by openly celebrating small wins along the way and maintaining your realistic optimism. See the Realistic Optimist. See the Humorist.

Maintain your resilience. Challenging the status quo can be tiring, even exhausting. Sometimes, it can be depressing and discouraging when things don't go as planned. Be aware of how you are feeling

and increase your resilience through any of the other Resiliator superpowers.

Remember: knowing that your questions can lead to better things increases your resilience.

Read the book below.

Reading

Rebels at Work: A Handbook for Leading Change From Within by Lois Kelly and Carmen Medina

Links

Rebels at Work – https://www.rebelsatwork.com

The Believer

Superpower: Believing

Believers are confident in their own abilities and are resilient as a result.

Believing in yourself is at the heart of resilience. Self-efficacy is about having the strong, positive belief that you have the capacity and the skills to achieve your goals.

Psychologist, Albert Bandura, defined self-efficacy as "one's belief in one's ability to succeed in specific situations or accomplish a task."

According to Bandura's social cognitive theory, people with high self-efficacy—that is, those who believe they can perform well—are more likely to view difficult tasks as something to be mastered rather than something to be avoided.

Self-efficacy is the optimistic self-belief in our ability to successfully accomplish a task and produce a favorable outcome. It is a belief that through hard work or learning or practice, we can succeed.

Individuals with self-efficacy are more likely to trust their own abilities when faced with constant change. They don't view problems as threats but see them as opportunities for growth and development.

Bandura names four sources of efficacy beliefs.

Mastery Experiences

The experience of mastering tasks increases our self-efficacy. Being successful at something increases our self-efficacy while failing at something decreases it. The secret here is setting small and incremental goals to maintain motivation and enable mastery of the task over time.

Vicarious Experiences

Watching other people, similar to you, is an important source of self-efficacy. When others succeed through sustained effort, it leads to your belief that you can do the same.

Verbal Persuasion

Other people, such as friends and colleagues, can strengthen your beliefs that you have what it takes to succeed. Being persuaded that we possess the capabilities to master certain activities means we are more likely to put in the effort and sustain it when problems arise.

Emotional and Psychological States

Your emotional and psychological state will influence how you perceive your self-efficacy.

If you are nervous, you may start to doubt yourself and decrease your self-efficacy. If you don't feel anxious or nervous, you may feel excited and increase your self-efficacy.

Depression, stress and anxiety will all have an influence on how you feel about your ability to succeed.

Being able to reduce or control negative emotions, such as stress, can have a positive impact on self-efficacy beliefs.

In their words

Maria's story

I didn't know how many superpowers I had until I was introduced to the Resiliator.

One of my superpowers is the Believer. I have used the Believer along with the Explorer.

I believe I have the ability to accomplish a task and achieve a goal through perseverance and persistence. I believe that success comes through hard work. I see achievement of difficult tasks as an opportunity for growth.

Data analytics was a big gap in my marketing skillset. I knew I would be unable to obtain a senior position in marketing without this skill. My adversity to numbers meant that was going to be a tough challenge. I approached it by setting myself small learning goals. It was only when I felt comfortable with my knowledge in a particular area that I moved on and set myself a new goal. Once I felt I had mastered data capture, I moved on to data integrity. Once I had mastered that, I moved on to descriptive analytics.

By setting small goals, I maintained my motivation and increased my self-efficacy and resilience.

 **Actions**

Start small. Don't set yourself up for failure by planning goals that could take forever to achieve. If you want to run a marathon, you don't set out on your first outing to run 42 kilometers. You set goals, build up the distance over time and award yourself each time you achieve the next goal. By setting interim goals, you increase self-efficacy and resilience. This is about *Mastery Experiences.*

Observe. Observe the success of your role models. You can perform the same task by imitation and sustained effort. This observation can result in mastery. This is about *Vicarious Experiences.*

Get support. When other people encourage and convince you to perform a task, you gain the belief that you are capable. So spend time with people who will support and encourage you. This is *Verbal Persuasion.*

Manage emotions. Your emotional reactions to situations play an important role in self-efficacy. Moods, emotional states, physical reactions and stress levels can all impact on how you feel about your capability in a particular situation. Therefore, if you can find strategies to minimize stress in challenging situations, you can improve your self-efficacy. This is about *Emotional and Psychological States.*

 **Reading**

The Power of Self-Efficacy: How to Believe in Yourself All the Way to Success by Justine Gantt

Self-Efficacy: The Exercise of Control by Albert Bandura

🌐 **Links**

Albert Bandura - http://www.professoralbertbandura.com

The Realistic Optimist

Superpower: Realistic Optimism

The Realistic Optimist believes that things can change for the better.

Optimism helps increase resilience by reducing stress.

But optimism is not about having your head in the clouds and hoping things will turn out okay. This is the idealistic optimist. The idealistic optimist believes that success will come to them if they just visualize it hard enough.

On the other hand, the Realistic Optimist believes they will succeed, but only with hard work, planning and persistence. They don't visualize an easy path to success; they think seriously about probable obstacles and how to overcome them.

The realistic optimist is positive and pragmatic. While they believe that things can change for the better, they also recognize that effort is involved. They know they can shoot for the stars but they will not lose sight of the ground.

The Realistic Optimist can make a real difference. When pessimists face challenges or obstacles, they give up. When the Realistic Optimist faces challenges or obstacles, they try harder. They propel themselves toward it, and find ways to overcome it and achieve their goals.

When you are an optimist, you think, feel and behave in a way that creates conditions for success.

Psychologist Gabriele Oettingen performed research on positive thinking and realistic optimism in 1991.[14] She asked 25 over-weight women, who had enrolled in a weight loss program, how likely they were to reach their goal. She found that those who were confident of success lost 26 pounds more than the self-doubters. Interestingly, the women who believed they would achieve their goal within a short period, lost 24 pounds less than those who recognized that the weight loss journey was going to take considerable effort.

This tells us that those who recognize that the road to success is a hard one are more likely to succeed. This is because it forces us to take action and plan how to navigate the obstacles we find along the way.

Realistic optimism can be nurtured. You can do this by having a positive attitude and combining that with a candid assessment of the problems and challenges that might await you. It is visualizing the success and the steps you will take to achieve that success.

Realistic optimism protects you from giving up when the going gets tough. If something gets in your way, you have the confidence to knuckle down and look for a solution.

There are other benefits. Research has shown that feeling positive can increase productivity and enhance cognitive skills. This is because your disposition affects how the brain operates. When you are feeling low,

the brain closes down while it focuses on what is wrong and how to get rid of it. When you are engaged, the brain opens up and you can enter a creative and innovative state.

The good news is that optimism, like all the superpowers, can be learned.

In their words

Taya's story

When the new customer relationship management (CRM) system was introduced to the contact center, it was very stressful. Initially, all I could see was doom and gloom. The call volumes were increasing due to the time of year, and I was still learning my way around the new system.

The Realistic Optimist superpower enabled me to take a different perspective. Rather than being a pessimist, I made the decision to be an optimist with the understanding that I would succeed through the application of hard work.

I knew that the new CRM would make a significant difference to the customer experience and that it would make my job much easier once I had mastered it. I applied myself to learn the new system and avoided distractions.

As I learned how the system worked, and saw and experienced the benefits, I focused on these things—the things that were working rather than the things that were not working.

If learning a particular aspect of the system took me longer than I expected, I didn't let it get me down. I maintained my realistic optimism throughout. When I did master a particular aspect, I had a little celebration with myself.

Realistic optimism gave me a fresh outlook and the speed at which I mastered the new system increased accordingly. My brain seemed to open up and click into a learning state and focus on accomplishment rather than failure.

Realistic optimism reduced my stress and anxiety and furnished me with a positive and pragmatic attitude.

Actions

Here is how you can become a realistic optimist.

Rather than focusing on things that are not working, focus on things that are working.

Surround yourself with more realistic optimists. Pessimism is contagious.

Look at things through a positive lens rather than a negative one. See the Reframer.

Identify the goal you want to achieve. It should be an attainable goal, even if it is a stretch one. For example, if you are color blind, your chances of becoming a doctor or a pilot are slim, so don't make that a goal.

Visualize achievement of the goal, what success looks like, and how that will make you feel.

Think about the challenges and obstacles you may face along the way.

Think about the steps you can take to overcome the challenges and obstacles. Make a plan.

On the journey, don't get depressed about bad situations. Find a pleasant distraction to take your mind off the situation. Then come

back to the situation with a problem-solving attitude and refer back to your plan. See the Solver.

Maintain a sense of humor. Humor can give you a new perspective about the problems and challenges you face. You can't be a victim if you are laughing. See the Humorist.

Look after yourself. Eat well and sleep well. Exercise and meditate.

Celebrate successes along the way. See the Celebrant.

Celebrate the achievement of your goal.

Identify the next goal you want to achieve. Rinse and repeat.

 Reading

Rethinking Positive Thinking: Inside the New Science of Motivation by Gabriele Oettingen

*Unfu*k Yourself: Get out of Your Head and Into Your Life* by Gary John Bishop

Learned Optimism: How to Change Your Mind and Your Life by Martin E. P. Seligman

Links

TED Talk: The Optimism Bias by Tali Sharot
https://www.ted.com/talks/tali_sharot_the_optimism_
bias?utm_campaign=tedspread&utm_medium=referral&utm_
source=tedcomshare

The Adapter

Superpower: Adaptation

The Adapter is resilient because they are flexible when change and uncertainly are present.

In a volatile, uncertain, complex and ambiguous world of constant change, the ability to continually adapt is a vital competency. Adaptability is key for individuals and organizations in need of a rapid response to constant change.

Non-adaptive behavior will kill an organization. Success comes from the ability of the people within it to adapt to new ways of thinking and working and to do so cohesively while remaining calm, attentive and confident.

A 2016 *Harvard Business Review Analytic Services* global survey identified *the ability to adapt* as the most important skill for organizations undergoing a digital transformation. The report stated:

Reflecting the strategic impetus currently driving digital transformations, technology knowledge is falling toward the bottom of the list of the skills that companies deem most important. The skills most in demand—the ability to adapt to change, customer-focused problem-solving, and collaboration and communication skills—underscore the growing focus on competitive capabilities and the barriers businesses face using technology to strengthen their competitive strength.[15]

Being adaptable reduces anxiety and stress. When you can anticipate and be ready for change, you can modify your attitude and expectations accordingly. Change doesn't need to throw you; it just becomes the way of life.

You can adapt your thinking and coping style and respond to events rather than react to them.

Being adaptable means you are open to new ideas: you are able to work independently or as part of a team; you are able to effectively multi-task through prioritization; and you can change direction along the way.

When you are adaptable, you will get more recognition and trust. You are not seen as the person who panics in the face of change. When you are adaptable, you respond to change better. You don't fear it. When you are adaptable, you will grow because you will take on new challenges. Successful people adapt whenever and wherever they need.

In their words

Maria's story

I absolutely had to get out of my comfort zone and become competent with data analytics. The Adapter superpower was fundamental in enabling me to do that.

I knew I had to engage in activities outside of my comfort zone if I were going to advance my marketing career.

I took small iterative steps. I knew I had to continually adapt to a changing world and that learning a new skill and capability was just one step along the way.

I knew that if I wanted to keep my career on track, I would have to sense and respond. I would have to observe what was happening in my profession and around me and be ahead of the game. Adaptation was paramount. I needed to embrace change, not resist it, if I were going to grow.

I had the willingness to adapt as it served my motivation, which was to progress my marketing career and obtain more senior positions.

Actions

Get out of your comfort zone. We can become adaptable when we engage in activities outside of our comfort zone. When we practice this in small steps, our comfort zone grows bigger and bigger. The bigger your comfort zone becomes, the more adaptable you will be. When you step outside your comfort zone, it does not have to be to face a major challenge. In fact, it is more likely that you will become adaptable if you practice it in small steps. This could be joining a working group to which you have previously said no or putting your hand up to facilitate the next team meeting.

Look at things from a different perspective. See the Reframer.

Sense and respond. In order to effectively adapt, you have to be able to do it as fast as or faster than the pace of change. Therefore, it is important to observe what is happening around you so you can be on the front foot. The more you observe, the more likely you are to anticipate outcomes and adapt quickly. We need to develop a sense-and-respond capability.

Sensing means being highly aware of what is going on and removing any filters that are confusing or altering what is really happening. These filters could be organizational or personal. Organizational filters could include inflated metrics, inaccessible information or red tape. Personal filters could include our own unconscious biases.

Responding means that we can adapt to the 'real' situation in the most beneficial manner.

Find your motivation. Adaptability starts with a willingness to adapt. This is difficult to do if you are not motivated to do so. Therefore, determine what motivates you and see adaptability through the motivational lens. For example, if learning and development motivates you, see adaptability through the lens of an opportunity for personal improvement.

Develop a growth mindset and grit. See the Explorer.

 Reading

The Platinum Rule: Discover the Four Basic Business Personalities and How They Can Lead You to Success by Tony Alessandra and Michael J. O'Connor

The Practice of Adaptive Leadership: Tools and Tactics for Changing Your Organization and the World by Ronald A. Heifetz and Marty Linsky

 Links

TEDxStCharles Adaptive Leadership-Leading Change by Marty Linksky
https://www.youtube.com/watch?v=af-cSvnEExM

The Achiever

Superpower: Achievement

The Achiever has a sense of purpose. Having a sense of purpose helps you overcome obstacles, which is essential to being resilient. A sense of purpose is your driver and feeds your intrinsic motivation. It gives your work, which is a large part of your life, meaning. Having a sense of purpose increases your engagement in the workplace, which in turn, reduces stress.

We all need to work, and sometimes we are not in the job we love. We should always look for that job, but in the meantime, we need to stay in the job we have. Well, all is not lost. According to researchers Jane E. Dutton and Amy Wrzesniewski, you *can* find a sense of purpose in your current job. The result of their extensive research was published in *The Academy of Management Review* in 2001.[16]

They coined the term 'job crafting', which is about turning the job you have into a job you love. Job crafting involves redefining your job to incorporate your values and beliefs, and strengths and passions.

There are three parts to job crafting and you can chose to do one or all of them. It involves rethinking the tasks, rethinking the people and rethinking the perceptions. It is all about assessing and altering aspects of your work.

Rethink the task

This is about rethinking the things you do at work, which is also known as task crafting. This is the process of adding tasks, emphasizing tasks or redesigning tasks. You can add tasks you enjoy into your job. For example, you may have an interest in communication and collaboration, so you add active participation on the organizations collaboration platform as a regular task.

If you already have tasks that you enjoy, you can emphasize them by devoting more time and energy to them.

Redesigning tasks means you look for ways to re-engineer existing tasks to make them more meaningful. For example, you may suggest that a new employee shadows you when you undertake a particular task. This adds more meaning to the task.

Although it may not be feasible for everyone to undertake task crafting, unless you do the assessment you won't know if there is room to maneuver. You may not be able to pick up new tasks and drop old ones altogether but you may be able to change them in some way.

Rethink the people

You can craft your interactions with others at work in ways that foster meaningfulness through altering with whom and how you form connections and relationships. Connections are short-term interactions that can develop into relationships. These relationships provide meaningfulness.

You can cultivate meaningfulness by building relationships with others who enable you to feel a sense of pride, dignity or worth. For example, researchers found that when hospital cleaners increased the amount of interaction they had with patients and their families, they did so because within these interactions they experienced more appreciation and enacted a role of caregiver, which elevated the sense of meaningfulness they derived from their work.[17]

You can reframe a relationship to create meaningfulness. For example, with your colleagues and peers, you can reframe the relationship and get to know more about their individual work preferences and interests, while also getting them to understand yours. This can change the nature of interactions, increase the quality of those interactions and provide more meaning to your role.

You can adapt relationships instead of changing the purpose or adding new ones. You can adapt existing relationships by providing more support and assistance to others, which in turn, can encourage others to do the same.

Rethink the perception

The third part of job crafting is creating meaningfulness in regards to how you think about your job.

You can expand your perceptions. You can increase meaningfulness by broadening your perception of the impact or purpose of your job. Think about your job as a whole, rather than a set of separate tasks and relationships. By seeing the bigger picture, you are able to see more meaning in the job.

You can focus your perception. You can find meaningfulness by narrowing your mental scope on specific tasks and relationships that are significant or valuable to you. This is useful if you dislike a substantial portion of your tasks or relationships, but you find particular parts of your job to be meaningful.

You can also link perceptions. You can take advantage of existing components of your job by drawing mental connections between specific tasks or relationships and interests, outcomes, or aspects of their identities that are meaningful to you. For example, if you have a passion for stand-up comedy, you might make a mental connection between performing comedy with moments in your work day when you joke with a customer to build rapport.

In their words

Aditya's story

There was a time when I lost my sense of purpose working in the finance department. I think it was because I had been there for a considerable time performing the same role. The lack of purpose led me to be disengaged, unmotivated and stressed. My resilience was lessened as a result.

The Achiever superpower enabled me to regain my sense of purpose and motivation. I read more about crafting a job and realized that I could find a sense of purpose in what I was doing. I made a list of all the tasks that my job entailed and flagged the ones that I really enjoyed.

My passion was in financial analysis. Financial analysts assemble financial reports and do forecasts of incoming revenue; they also run business studies.

Although it wasn't originally a major component of my job, I agreed with my manager that I could take on more financial analysis and alleviate the workload of my colleagues. In exchange, a colleague took over some of my compliance work.

I took on as much financial analysis as I could because I enjoyed it and I am good at it. I have now become the go-to person for financial analysis and I love my job so much more because of it.

I also crafted my interactions with others. I built relationships with people in the departments who were recipients of my financial analysis. I thought of them as my customers. I was able to find out how I could improve what I delivered to them and, as a result, I felt a sense of pride when I delivered them a better service.

Actions

Practice job crafting to create a sense of purpose and achievement.

Obtain a copy of a job-crafting tool. See link below.

Reading

Alive at Work: The Neuroscience of Helping Your People Love What They Do by Daniel M. Cable

How to Be Happy at Work: The Power of Purpose, Hope and Friendships by Annie McKee

Links

Job crafting tool - https://jobcrafting.com

Crafting a Job: Revisiong Employees as Active Crafters of Their Work - https://www.researchgate.net/publication/211396297_Crafting_a_Job_Revisioning_Employees_as_Active_Crafters_of_Their_Work

The Celebrant

Superpower: Celebration

The Celebrant celebrates both successes and failures.

Successes

If we celebrate successes, we can develop a success mindset. Celebrating success is one way of cultivating this mindset. Celebrate successes no matter how small. Don't get overwhelmed by what is left to be done; instead, stop and celebrate what you have achieved.

Keep telling yourself "I have succeeded", "I am an achiever", "I can do this because I have done it before and succeeded." Be proud of what you have done.

When you celebrate successes, you increase your motivation and resilience.

If you have large goals, break them down into smaller tasks or actions that you can celebrate once you have achieved them.

When we anticipate success or achieve success and celebrate, we release dopamine into our brain. This feels good and we want more. Dopamine contributes to feelings of pleasure and satisfaction as part of the reward system.

When we celebrate successes openly, it gives others the chance to join in and feel motivated.

Failures

Thomas Edison said, "I have not failed. I've just found 10,000 ways that won't work."

If you have found 10,000 ways that don't work, you have learned from your mistakes and are better able to see what will work. Every time you fail, you are closer to success. It may not feel like it but you will be closer than you think.

When we fail, we often feel upset and disappointed or even frustrated. The problem with these feelings is they stop us from having another go so we feel real failure. If we celebrate failure as a learning opportunity and a step closer to success, we have the motivation to keep going. This is all about perseverance and resilience.

We should celebrate failure because the most successful people have failed. There is the famous quote from basketball legend Michael Jordon: "I've missed more than 9,000 shots in my career. I've lost almost 300 games. Twenty-six times, I've been trusted to take the game-winning shot and missed. I've failed over and over and over again in my life. And that is why I succeed."

Failure imparts experience, personal growth and development. Failure gives you the biggest dose of feedback. So celebrate it, it's a good thing.

In their words

Taya's story

Everyone in the contact center had felt some level of stress and anxiety during the implementation of the new customer relationship (CRM) system. All of us used the Resiliator superpowers to be more resilient in the constant change we were facing.

After the Christmas mayhem, I called upon the Celebrant superpower. We celebrated the successful implementation but also the successful adoption by contact center staff. We knew more change was coming, as more features of the new CRM were activated, but we wanted to celebrate even the small achievements along the way and cultivate the success mindset.

We sent a thank-you and recognition email to the IT support team who helped us while we were finding our way around the system. We patted each other on the back for a job well done. We had a celebratory drink after work. In fact, we did it twice to cover all the shifts and ensure no one missed out.

Actions

Pat it. When you have a success, pat yourself on the back and cultivate your success mindset.

Say it. Thank someone for doing a great job. Praise someone for doing something well or going the extra mile. If you do this in public, it makes the celebration greater and the other person feels recognized.

Write it. Send a person an email praising them for doing a great job. Even better, you can email the whole team with the praise for the individual.

Eat it: Hold a celebratory lunch for bigger wins.

Learn it. Learn from your failures and share the learning with others. Be aware of how you react to failure and create a plan to remove the negative responses. See the Regulator. Practice embracing failure and see it as a positive experience and a growth opportunity.

Post it. Create a fail wall (physical or virtual) where anyone can post their failure and what they learnt from it. Watch it grow. You can also create a kudos wall and post praise for colleagues.

Table it. Start every team meeting with a discussion of successes and failures.

 Reading

How to Be Resilient: The Blueprint for Getting Results When Things Don't Go to Plan by Stacey Copas

Happiness at Work: Be Resilient, Motivated, and Successful - No Matter What by Srikumar S. Rao

Option B: Facing Adversity, Building Resilience and Finding Joy by Sheryl Sandberg

Links

TED Talk: The unexpected benefit of celebrating failure by Astro Teller
https://www.ted.com/talks/astro_teller_the_unexpected_
benefit_of_celebrating_failure?utm_campaign=tedspread&utm_
medium=referral&utm_source=tedcomshare

The Humorist

Superpower: Humor

Humor is one of the most powerful tools you have when faced with constant change, stress and anxiety. You can't be a victim when you are laughing.

Research has shown that humor can alleviate depression and increase our physical and emotional well-being.[18] It improves mood, releases stress and anxiety; it allows the release of pent-up feelings of anger and frustration, and it affects behavior in a positive manner. When we are humorous, we increase our connection with others. We make more eye contact, increase our levels of communication, and we are more tactile.

The Humorist uses humor as a coping mechanism to prepare for stress and increase resilience.

Of course, there is a time, place and situation in which humor should be used. So there is caution. But that doesn't mean we shouldn't use it with consideration.

Self-depreciation is the safest form of humor and not only creates laughter but also makes you more approachable as you are showing your vulnerability. Make fun of your mistakes and weaknesses.

When you can laugh at adversity, you have already distanced yourself from it. You have become an observer of the situation. When you have that psychological distance, you are in a better position to acknowledge your negative emotions and chose alternative responses that are positive and help you to cope.

Humor can broaden your focus of attention and, as a result, it can promote exploration, creativity, innovation and flexibility in thinking.

Humor, and the ability to clear your head, can help you avoid becoming stuck in feelings of negativity and helplessness so you're better able to see the bigger picture and move forward.

Humor is good for individuals and it can improve the culture within an organization. Humor helps colleagues connect with each other because shared humor can improve overall morale, motivation, creativity and innovation.

Laughter is the best medicine.

In their words

Maria's story

I think humor is one of the most important superpowers the Resiliator has. I use the Humorist when I am feeling overwhelmed or stressed. I used it when I had to master data analytics because I wanted to progress my career in marketing.

My learning program was self-paced so I wasn't under time pressure. The pressure I felt was self-induced, as I wanted to learn faster than I was able. When I felt the pressure, I would use the Humorist to laugh at myself with others. I would laugh at "the crazy person" who hated numbers but who was trying to master data analytics at the speed of a mathematics prodigy.

I found that when I could see the humor in something, I could adopt the role of an observer. This put a bit of distance between me and the cause of my stress. It made me take a step back and focus on the positive such as how much I had already learned.

The humorist helped me clear my mind and not get dragged down into negative thoughts about the learning curve I was navigating.

Sharing the humor of the situation gave me the support of others, which increased my motivation to succeed. I was able to move forward having taken a psychological step back.

Actions

Smile more. Research has shown that a smile, even a fake one, can release endorphins that make you feel happier. It reduces stress.

Laugh at yourself. Don't be so hard on yourself. Self-depreciation creates laughter and makes you more approachable.

Reframe. View the situation though a different lens—one with a sprinkling of humor. See the Reframer.

Share. Share your frustrations with others and laugh about them together.

 Reading

The Resilient Self by Steven J. Wolin and Sybil Wolin

You Can't Be Serious: Taking Humor to Work by Michael Kerr

The Humor Advantage: Why Some Businesses Are Laughing All the Way to the Bank by Michael Kerr

Humor: The Lighter Path to Resilience and Health by Paul McGhee

Links

TEDxTemecula Laughter is the Best Medicine by David Cruz
- https://youtu.be/PlMrpfviozk

The Futurist

Superpower: Futuring

The Futurist maintains a long-term perspective and avoids seeing stressful situations as all-encompassing and overwhelming. The Futurist knows that it will pass.

They see a situation in a broader context. They avoid blowing everything out of proportion.

You might not be able to change a current situation, but you can look to the future and perceive how things might improve. Dwelling on the current situation increases stress and decreases resilience.

There is nothing wrong with the statement "live in the moment" but if that moment is a bad one, you should look to the future to get through it.

The Futurist also does not dwell on the negative things that have happened in the past. The Futurist puts them where they belong—in the past—and moves on. They learn from the situation but don't allow it to cultivate negative emotions.

If you can envision a future where you are not stressed and anxious about what you are experiencing in the present, you can get through it. You can reduce the intensity of the negative emotions and the angst being experienced.

Try to place yourself in the future and look back at your current situation—this can put the current situation into perspective and it may not look so bad. Distancing yourself is a good psychological method for increasing resilience.

When we can anticipate a better future and envisage something to look forward to, we can feel happier and less stressed before the future arrives (no matter how we feel in the present).

Being able to look to the future is an essential quality for resilience.

Backcasting

The Futurist uses a technique called backcasting. Backcasting is the process of defining a desired future state then working backwards to identify what needs to take place to get there.

It is different from forecasting in that forecasting works forward from a current state based on what we know. Backcasting approaches the challenge of discussing the future from the opposite direction.

The Futurist will take a long-term perspective and determine what the ideal future could look like. This could be five, ten or 20 years into the future. The technique looks beyond the current state (and its risks and constraints) and imagines a future that is informed by the past but is not an extension of it.

Backcasting drives creativity and innovation. It builds resilience because the long-term perspective can be envisioned without constraints of current products, services, resources, processes or technology etc.

Backcasting starts with the identification of current issues and problems. Then it envisions a future where those issues and problems have been resolved. Steps to achieving this future are determined: actions, assumptions, risks, benefits and any other indicators that would help achieve the future state.

In their words

Aditya's story

The Futurist superpower is one I have used in conjunction with others such as the Collaborator and the Questioner. I used the Collaborator to determine the best way to increase financial awareness across the organization, and I used the Questioner to introduce new ways of working and thinking into the finance department.

Neither of those initiatives where going to be completed in the short term. While I was eager to make a difference, I was also frustrated with the time it was going to take to bring about change; however, I didn't let it encompass and overwhelm me.

The Futurist enabled me to keep a long-term perspective and focus on what the future would look like when the changes came about.

Looking to the future increased my resilience.

Actions

Leave the past where it is. It is in the past.

Remember that the present is temporary and will pass. Look to the future.

Think back to a stressful event you experienced and how you felt post that event. At the time, it was overwhelming and all-encompassing, but after the event, it wasn't that bad.

Practice backcasting

In its simplest form, a backcasting session can run as follows:

1. If possible, obtain an experienced facilitator who is familiar with backcasting.

2. Find a location with a large wall or table for placement of a large number of sticky notes. For remote teams, use a virtual whiteboard or other collaboration platform supporting the use of sticky notes for brainstorming.

3. Invite stakeholders.

4. Set the timeline: how far into the future are we projecting?

5. Baseline current state: identify current issues and problems and agree what is going to be targeted.

6. Define possible future states / scenarios where issues and problems have been resolved.

7. Brainstorm. Work backwards (to the present) and identify the actions, assumptions, risks and benefits (and other indicators) to reach the future state. Capture these on sticky notes. Different colors may be used for different indicators.

8. Capture the outcomes then assess the options and select the best option with the goal of creating an actionable plan including risk and threat mitigation.

9. Establish and put into place an implementation plan.

10. Conduct this activity on a regular basis.

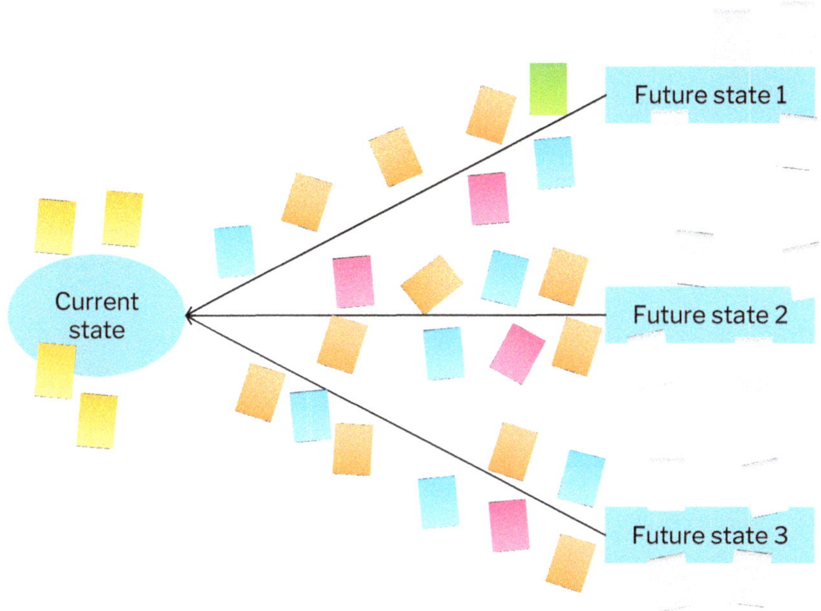

 # Reading

The Resiliency Advantage by Al Siebert

 # Links

Forecasting and Backcasting - Design Defined | Bresslergroup
https://www.bresslergroup.com/blog/design-defined-forecasting-
and-backcasting/

The Thanker

Superpower: Thankfulness

The Thanker has gratitude for everything that has got them to where they are today as opposed to focusing on the obstacles in front of them.

We tend to only see what is in front of us and we take for granted those things that are behind us.

Researchers, Davidai and Gilovich, published a paper titled *The Headwinds/Tailwinds Asymmetry: An Availability Bias in Assessments of Barriers and Blessings.*[19]

In this paper, they acknowledge that having gratitude has many benefits including:

•   Increased resilience

- Increased energy
- Improved sleep
- Mental toughness
- Better physical health
- Improved self-esteem
- Improved relationships.

Robert Emmons is a professor of psychology at the University of California.[20] He has authored two books about gratitude and says that even in the worst times, being grateful can help us through them. It can energize, heal and bring hope.

It is hard to understand how gratitude could come naturally during a crisis but Emmons points out that we need to make the vital distinction between 'feeling' grateful and 'being' grateful.

We cannot always control our emotions—our feelings.

But being grateful is a choice. When the going gets tough, gratitude provides us with a perspective from which we can see the bigger picture—life in its entirety. This can stop us becoming overwhelmed by present and temporary circumstances.

Gaining this perspective may not come easy but continually having a go has enormous benefits. If we can think of the worst times and remember that we made it through, we can be grateful.

Gratitude gives us the power to change an obstacle into an opportunity and a loss into a potential gain.

You have the ability to experience genuine gratitude in the face of your challenges but it is your choice whether you do so. Remember, gratitude is a cornerstone of resilience.

In their words

Charlie's story

Thankfulness is so important in terms of resilience. When I was promoted to team lead in the distribution department, I was overwhelmed by the task ahead of me. I wanted to be the best leader I could and I was also cognizant that there was an enormous amount of change happening.

My team members were facing change in processes and systems. I knew I would have to help them and me to be resilient. It was too easy to get overwhelmed by what was ahead of me and just see the obstacles. I used the Thanker superpower and felt gratitude for what had got me to where I was in that moment.

I was thankful for my manager who was tremendously supportive of my development and saw the potential in me as a team leader.

I was thankful for the education and learning opportunities I had been given to improve my leadership skills.

I was thankful for the support of my team who welcomed me into the position as their team leader.

I was thankful for my colleagues who boosted my confidence with their positivity and encouragement.

As I reflected on all the things I was thankful for, I could feel my energy and resilience increase.

I also wondered if these people actually knew the extent of my gratitude. I wrote a letter of thanks to each of them. Engaging in that act of gratitude further increased my energy and resilience, and improved my relationships. The Thanker was, and continues to be, my keystone superpower.

Actions

Keep a gratitude journal. Keep a daily journal of things for which you are grateful. This acts as an affirmation of good things.

Engage in acts of gratitude. Thank others verbally or in writing, or both.

Reframe the situation. See the Reframer.

Practice mindfulness. See the Observer.

 # Reading

Thanks!: How Practicing Gratitude Can Make You Happier by Robert Emmons

Gratitude Works!: A 21-Day Program for Creating Emotional Prosperity by Robert Emmons

Links

How Gratitude Changes You and Your Brain - https://greatergood.berkeley.edu/article/item/how_gratitude_changes_you_and_your_brain

The Revealer

Superpower: Revelation

The Revealer turns up as their authentic self.

We often try to be someone other than our real selves. We have a skewed view that we need to adopt a persona so that others will like us or respect us.

We engage in self-presentation and modify our behaviors, emotions and the way we are seen by others. We can do it for many reasons. We may not feel we can express ourselves freely. We may feel that we have to have all the answers or we will lose credibility.

However, the energy you put in to pretending to be someone else is exhausting. It diminishes both your energy and your resilience. Trying to be someone you are not is not sustainable.

Being your authentic self is when everything you do is aligned with your goals, your values, your beliefs and your moral compass.

The Revealer reveals their true self. This may make you feel vulnerable and you may feel that it will be seen as a weakness. However, vulnerability looks like courage to everyone else.

Being your authentic self at work doesn't mean that you go to work in gym gear or ripped jeans. Authenticity isn't about what you wear; it is about who you are at the core.

When you are afraid to speak up in a meeting or pretend to understand something that you don't understand at all, you are not being true to yourself. You are not being authentic.

We have to be prepared to bring our authentic self to the workplace. We have to be our whole self at work. This means we are humble and vulnerable, and we recognize that we are not perfect.

When we are authentic, we have the courage to ask questions, admit when we don't understand, ask for help, and make genuine connections with others. This, most likely, will not come easy. It can be scary. The voices in your head will tell you that you will get shot down and that no-one will listen: What if they don't like what I say? What if it diminishes my career progression?

We have to stop listening to those voices and be true to ourselves. We have to take a risk and believe that we are better than those voices.

We have to stop avoiding situations because we fear we will make mistakes or fail. To be authentic, we must face those fears and feelings and deliberately step out of our comfort zone. We must accept that we will experience fear but observe it as a natural response and not as a reflection on our lack of ability. When we do this, we can radically reduce the negative impact.

Studies have shown that being authentic reduces stress and increases resilience. Being authentic can improve job satisfaction, engagement, and performance.[21]

In their words

Charlie's story

When I was given the team leader position, I knew I absolutely had to use the Revealer superpower. It was something I had to keep reminding myself of every day. I wanted to be the best leader I could be but was also aware that I was on a steep learning curve. This was my first leadership role (with a title).

It would be easy to pretend I had all the answers; to pretend that I was a fully competent leader; to pretend that I would not make mistakes; to pretend that the job was going to be a walk in the park; to pretend that I had this sorted 100%.

Sometimes, I felt the team was looking at me for all the answers. I had to be authentic and share with my team what I did know as well as what I didn't know.

Whenever I felt myself hiding behind a façade, I made a note so I could later reflect on the moment and determine what had triggered it. Being aware of the triggers meant I could avoid the lack of authenticity.

Being authentic with my team members and showing my vulnerability actually improved our relationship. They saw my acknowledgement of not having all the answers and that I was learning just as they were, as signs of strength not weakness.

I think the Revealer can be one of the hardest superpowers to master as it can make you feel exposed, but with practice, it can become your greatest strength.

 Actions

Keep a journal about each time you are not being your authentic self.

Look for trends and triggers when you are not your whole self.

Admit when you don't know something.

Acknowledge when you have made a mistake.

Ask for help.

 Reading

Bring Your Whole Self to Work: How Vulnerability Unlocks Creativity, Connection, and Performance by Mike Robbins

Links

How To Be Yourself - Become Your Authentic Self Right Now by Actualized.org
- https://www.youtube.com/watch?v=w1JzhhDMcpw

The Reframer

Superpower: Reframing

The Reframer is able to look at a situation in more than one way. When we experience an event, we generally make an initial assumption and interpretation of that event. This is a frame.

The Reframer looks at the event from different perspectives. They take a situation observed from one angle and view if from another angle to give it more context. This is a reframe.

The Reframer looks to remove negativity from their perspective and increase the positivity by looking for opportunities.

Often, we cannot control what happens to us but we can control how we respond to it.

A great example of reframing is the story of Tom Watson, the founder of IBM. Watson was aware that one of his employees had made a mistake that cost the organization 10 million dollars. The employee was asked to meet Watson in his office. As the employee entered the office he said, "I suppose you want my resignation?"

Watson looked at him and said in disbelief, "Are you kidding? We have just spent 10 million dollars on your education."

In this reframe, Watson recognized that the mistake had already occurred, and that the money had already been lost but the situation could be seen as an opportunity to recover some value from this employee.

When we ask if the glass is half full or half empty, both answers are correct. They are just different perspectives. The Reframer could add another perspective and say it is neither half full nor half empty—it is full. The glass contains 50% liquid and 50% air; therefore, it is full.

Reframing forces us to be more focused, creative and innovative. It forces us to stand back and see things differently. It increases our resilience in the face of constant change.

Imagine standing on the edge of the platform in the subway. As the train comes through the station at close proximity, the velocity pushes you backward like a shock wave. It is disturbing. But when you stand farther back, the speed of the train seems much slower, and it is much less disturbing. So, depending on where you are standing—your vantage point—your perceptions of events and change can be quite different.

In summary, reframing allows us to see something in a different way, in a context that enables us to recognize and appreciate that there are positive aspects to the current situation. Reframing allows us to take onboard whatever has happened and find opportunities rather than problems.

Reframing is not oblivious to the fact that events we encounter are often difficult, dramatic and disruptive. But rather than succumb to them and view them as rejection, hardship, damaging and destructive, we have the choice to reframe them.

"Change how you see and see how you change."—Zen proverb

Wonder over worry

Author, Amber Rae, coined the term 'wonder over worry'. The Reframer chooses whether to see a challenge as a worry or a wonder.

Unfortunately, our brains are hardwired to give more focus to negative experiences than positive ones. This was crucial, in ages gone by, when survival was of the upmost concern while hunting for food in tiger infested jungles. Our focus needed to be on the negative experiences.

Research has shown that negative thoughts stimulate the areas of the brain that promote depression and anxiety. Positive thoughts stimulate the areas that result in feelings of calm and peace.[22]

The Reframer knows that we can train our brains to wonder rather than worry. The Reframer takes a moment to pause, step back and reframe a situation by being curious.

We can choose to allow the default mode of negativity to take over or to reframe and see things through a curious and positive lens.

In their words

Taya's story

The new customer relationship management (CRM) system in the contact center freaked me out. It was introduced at a busy time of year. It was taking me some time to get used to its navigation and interfaces with other systems.

All I could see were issues, and I viewed the whole experience of the CRM as negative. It all seemed too hard.

In addition to some other superpowers, I used the Reframer with some of my colleagues. We took our situation and wondered how we could look at it from a different perspective. We brainstormed ideas on how we could change our angle of view and find positives rather than dwell on the negatives.

One reframe was the realization that the CRM was leading technology and that once we had learned to use the system, it would be a massive drawcard on our résumés if, for any reason, we decided to leave the organization.

We also realized that as our organization was an early adopter, we could share our experience with other organizations; thus, raising the profile of the organization and ourselves.

The Reframer helped us see the opportunities the new CRM presented to us. Then we could see our learning as an opportunity and not an obstacle.

 Actions

Remember that your initial assessment of a situation may be wrong or not entirely correct.

Be attentive to the fact that even if your initial assessment does contain some correct information, you are probably still looking at the situation from a very limited view point.

Consider other ways in which to look at the situation. When you come up with new ideas, you are reframing.

Look for opportunities rather than problems, strengths rather than weaknesses, and view impossibilities as possibilities

 ## Reading

Reframe: Shift the Way You Work, Innovate, and Think by Mona Patel

Choose Wonder Over Worry: Move Beyond Fear and Doubt to Unlock Your Full Potential by Amber Rae

 ## Links

TEDxAthens Perspective is Everything by Rory Sutherland
https://www.ted.com/talks/rory_sutherland_perspective_is_everything?utm_campaign=tedspread&utm_medium=referral&utm_source=tedcomshare

The Listener

Superpower: Listening

Effective listening is critical to building and maintaining resilience. Effective listening can avoid misunderstanding, which in turn, leads to avoidance of conflict. Misunderstanding and conflict have no place in a resilient workforce.

Effective listening helps us to avoid jumping to unfounded conclusions and making assumptions. If we are to be truly resilient, we need to fully understand the context in which we find ourselves, the problem or challenge, and the options available. If we make assumptions, we will be off-kilter and make ill-informed decisions.

When we are under pressure and feeling stressed, it is easy to listen with emotional barriers in place and not really hear what is being said. Our emotions and unconscious biases can get in the way. These can translate what is being said into something quite different.

In a stressful environment, it can be easy to become distracted by what is going on around you and not hear a conversation in its entirety.

Effective communication and effective listening go hand-in-hand but as the saying goes "We have two ears and one mouth for a reason." This means we should use them in that proportion—we should listen twice as much as we speak.

Effective listening is the foundation for many of the other superpowers. For example:

- The Empathizer needs to use active (or empathetic) listening to receive and accurately understand what the other person is saying. This enables an appropriate response. Empathetic listening builds trust and respect and enables the speaker to release their emotions. It enables the listener to tune in to what it's really like from the other person's perspective.

- The Solver needs good listening skills. Listening is critical for problem- solving. The Solver needs to listen to all those who have a vested interest in the resolution, and focus on what each person has to say. When we listen, we can ask great questions and, therefore, gather as much information as possible about the problem or issue being faced.

- Listening and asking questions are of the upmost importance to the Collaborator. We have filters, biases and interpretative lenses, which means we sometimes only hear what we want to hear. It will inhibit effective collaboration if we are not able to take a step back from our own ideas to be open and fully understand the ideas of others.

- The Regulator has to undertake accurate self-assessment as they cannot change what they do not know. One way to do this is to ask for honest, constructive and candid feedback. When this feedback is given, it is paramount to be receptive to it without becoming defensive.

Effective listening means paying attention, demonstrating that you are really listening, validating what you are hearing and not making judgement.

Listening does not always come easy but it can be honed with practice. Listening can be hard when we have our own deep-rooted beliefs that can trigger a response within us. It can be hard when we are surrounded by distractions and diversions. Our state of mind and emotional disposition can also influence what we hear when someone is speaking.

Just like all the other superpowers, effective listening can be learned. The more you use the listening muscle, the stronger it will become.

In their words

Aditya's story

I used the Questioner superpower to introduce new ways of working and thinking into the finance department. I engaged people from other departments who had adopted more agile ways of working to talk to us about what they had done and the benefits they had realized.

I was very excited about the prospect of change, as were some of my colleagues. We were motivated and enthusiastic. We jumped to the conclusion that everyone would feel the same. We made a big assumption. I had not listened.

The Listener superpower made sure that I recognized the power of effective listening. Doing so would increase my resilience, and the resilience of others, as we didn't fall foul to misinterpretation or failed communication.

I needed to pay attention and "really" hear what people were saying, and to also call on the Empathizer superpower and see things from others' perspective.

Sometimes listening was hard. My enthusiasm and excitement to move on with the changes was distracting.

Effective listening ensured that I understood the fears and concerns of others and could take action to overcome them. With effective listening, we all went on the journey of change together and achieved remarkable outcomes, as a result.

 **Actions**

Try the following to become a more effective listener.

Pay attention

The person speaking should feel they have your full and undivided attention.

- Look directly at the person speaking.
- Avoid distractions.
- Do not prepare a response to what is being said.
- Be cognizant of the speaker's body language.

Body language

Your body language can demonstrate engagement with the speaker.

- Make eye contact.
- Nod occasionally.
- Keep an open and interested posture.
- Smile occasionally.
- Use small expressions or words like 'yes', 'ah-ha' etc. to encourage the speaker to keep talking.

Validate

It is important for the listener and the speaker to validate understanding. The listener needs to reflect on what has been said and validate their comprehension.

- Repeat what has been heard and ask if that is an accurate summation.
- Ask questions to seek further clarification but allow the speaker to finish speaking. Don't interrupt.

Open your mind

Defer judgement and keep an open mind. Do not interrupt the speaker with counter arguments.

Do not let your biases, judgements or opinions distract you from what is being said. Remember: what is being said, is the speaker's reality.

 ## Reading

Deep Listening: Impact Beyond Words by Oscar Trimboli

Listening Well: The Art of Empathic Understanding by William R. Miller

Links

TED 5 Ways to Listen Better – Julian Treasure
- https://www.youtube.com/watch?v=cSohjlYQI2A

Acknowledgments

135

My deep thanks go to:

Breed Barrett for her undying support, encouragement, contribution and patience.

Sylvie Blair at BookPOD for her ongoing help and guidance.

Jo Yardley at The Editing House for her attention to detail and excellence.

Peter Phan at Flimp Studios for the cover and illustrations and for bringing the Resiliator to life.

Working with Karen

You can engage Karen in the following ways:

Program Facilitator

- Unleash the Resiliator within – for leaders
- Unleash the Resiliator within – for individuals
- Change management coalition capability
- Change network enablement
- Adaptive leadership
- Adaptive leadership teams
- Leadership development optimized
- Need for speed – new tools for a new age
- Agile change management
- Leaders let go
- Change is everyone's business
- Creating a culture for innovation
- When everyone leads

Trainer

Training courses are available for all levels of your organization and are based on any of the programs.

Speaker

Keynote speaker for your next event based on any of the programs. Keynotes are tailored to your needs and those of your organization or audience.

Coach

Coaching for teams and individuals who need to evolve in line with the evolution of the business.

Coaching for change practitioners needing to revise their approach to align with the speed of change in the organization.

Coaching for leaders who need to become more effective and adaptive.

Mentor

Grow and learn through a mentoring relationship with Karen by sharing in her wisdom and experience.

Author

Contributing thought-provoking content for your next publication.

Connecting with Karen

139

Twitter:	@karen_ferris
LinkedIn:	https://www.linkedin.com/in/karenferris/
Facebook:	https://www.facebook.com/karenferristhoughtleaderOCM/
Instagram:	karenferrisdotcom

Endnotes

1   https://www.gallup.com/workplace/238079/state-global-workplace-2017.aspx

2   https://news.gallup.com/businessjournal/190445/negative-impact-disengaged-employees-germany.aspx

3   https://news.gallup.com/opinion/gallup/193490/unhappy-state-local-government-workers-cost-billions.aspx

4   https://www.talentforgrowth.com/engagement/disengaged-employees/

5   https://www.who.int/mental_health/in_the_workplace/en/

6   https://www.headsup.org.au/docs/default-source/resources/beyondblue_workplaceroi_finalreport_may-2014.pdf

7   https://www.who.int/mental_health/in_the_workplace/en/

8   https://www.victorianchamber.com.au/news-media/all/2019/11/workplace-manslaughter-laws-and-proposed-coverage

9   https://www.bbc.com/news/world-europe-50865211

10 http://www.creativeeducationfoundation.org/creative-problem-solving/the-cps-process/

11 The CPS Learners Model comprises the work of G.J. Puccio, M. Mance, M.C. Murdock, B. Miller, J. Vehar, R. Firestien, S. Thurber, & D. Nielsen.

12 http://www.creativeeducationfoundation.org

13   https://www.britannica.com/science/information-theory/Physiology

14   https://link.springer.com/article/10.1007%2FBF01173206

15 https://hbr.org/resources/pdfs/comm/genpact/AcceleratingPaceAndImpactofDigitalTransformation.pdf

16 http://faculty.som.yale.edu/amywrzesniewski/documents/Craftingajob_Revisioningemployees_000.pdf

17 https://link.springer.com/article/10.1007/s12186-017-9173-z

18 https://www.forbes.com/sites/daviddisalvo/2017/06/05/six-science-based-reasons-why-laughter-is-the-best-medicine/#614e8bd67f04

19 https://www.ncbi.nlm.nih.gov/pubmed/27869473

20 https://greatergood.berkeley.edu/profile/robert_emmons

21 https://www.researchgate.net/publication/292316233_SelfComplexity_and_the_Authenticity_of_Self_Aspects_Effects_on_Well_Being_and_Resilience_to_Stressful_Events

22 https://www.collabra.org/articles/10.1525/collabra.128/

References

Duckworth, A. (2017). *Grit: The Power of Passion and Perserverance.* London: Ebury Publishing.

Dweck, C. (2007). *Mindset: The New Psychology of Success.* New York: Ballentine Books.

Goleman, D. (2000). *Working With Emotional Intelligence.* Bantam.

Goleman, D. (2005). *Emotional Intelligence: Why It Matters More Than IQ.* Bantam Books.